WALKS IN THE CATHAR REGION
CATHAR CASTLES OF SOUTH WEST FRANCE

by
Alan Mattingly

2 POLICE SQUARE, MILNTHORPE, CUMBRIA LA7 7PY
www.cicerone.co.uk

© Alan Mattingly 2005
ISBN 1 85284 423 X

Photos: Alan Mattingly (unless otherwise acknowledged)

A catalogue record for this book is available from the British Library.

Acknowledgements

Special gratitude is due to all those, volunteers and professionals alike, who have recently planned, waymarked, maintained and written about the paths described in this book. Some have no doubt been motivated principally by a love of the outdoors; others by a desire to bring more tourists to their villages. But the result of their labours is a wonderful network of walking routes which is continually being added to and improved.

For their various measures of help, advice and patient tolerance I would also like to thank in particular: Branton Bamford, Hazel Clarke, Alan Haworth, Lucy Histed, Terry Marsh, Wendy Mattingly, David Monnet, Jim Palfrey, Eliane Pech, Sébastien Pla, Joseph Ribas and Jonathan Williams.

I am grateful as well to Stuart Alderman, former Chief Executive of Ramblers Holidays. A few years ago Stuart asked me to prepare a Ramblers Holidays walking tour in this part of France. That tour formed the starting point for the walks in this book.

My gratitude will be further extended to all readers who follow these walks and, on finding any problems or changes to the routes, tell me about them. Please send this information to the publisher by e-mail or otherwise

Advice to Readers

Readers are advised that while every effort is taken by the author to ensure the accuracy of this guidebook, changes can occur which may affect the contents. It is advisable to check locally on transport, accommodation, shops, etc, but even rights of way can be altered. The publisher would welcome notes of any such changes.

Front cover: *Quéribus – possibly the most vertiginous of all Cathar castles (Section 12)*

WALKS IN THE CATHAR REGION
CATHAR CASTLES OF SOUTH WEST FRANCE

About the Author

Alan Mattingly was Director of the Ramblers' Association from 1974 to 1998. At various times during that period he also held other posts in the outdoor and conservation movements in Britain, including that of Chairman of the Council for National Parks.

A member of the Outdoor Writers' Guild, he received that organisation's Golden Eagle Award in 1998. He is also a recipient of the John Hunt Award (from the Countrywide Holidays Association) and the Wildlife and Countryside Link Award. His previous publications include *Tackle Rambling* (1981) and *Walking in the National Parks* (1982).

He is now based in a small town in the eastern Pyrenees that lies just below the 2800m Pic du Canigou. When not exploring that most impressive and captivating of mountains on foot, he writes and teaches English.

(Photo by Branton Bamford)

CONTENTS

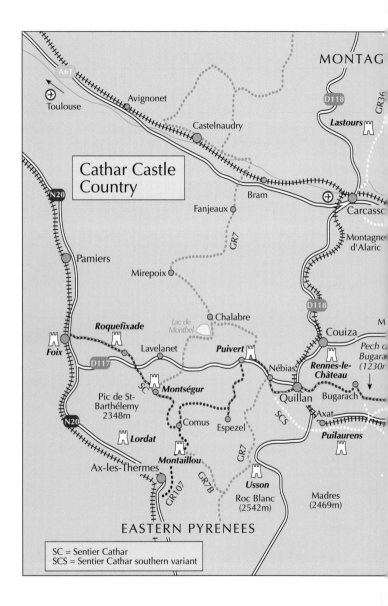

Cathar Castle Country

MONTAG

Toulouse

A61

Avignonet

Castelnaudry

D118

GR36

Lastours

N20

Bram

Fanjeaux

Carcassc

GR7

Carcassc

Montagne d'Alaric

Pamiers

Mirepoix

D118

Chalabre

Lac de Montbel

Couiza

M

Roquefixade

Puivert

Pech d Bugara (1230r

Foix

D117

Lavelanet

Nébias

Rennes-le-Château

SC

Montségur

Quillan

Bugarach

Pic de St-Barthélemy 2348m

Comus

Espezel

SCS

Axat

N20

Lordat

GR7

Puilaurens

Ax-les-Thermes

Montaillou

GR107

GR7B

Usson

Madres (2469m)

Roc Blanc (2542m)

EASTERN PYRENEES

SC = Sentier Cathar
SCS = Sentier Cathar southern variant

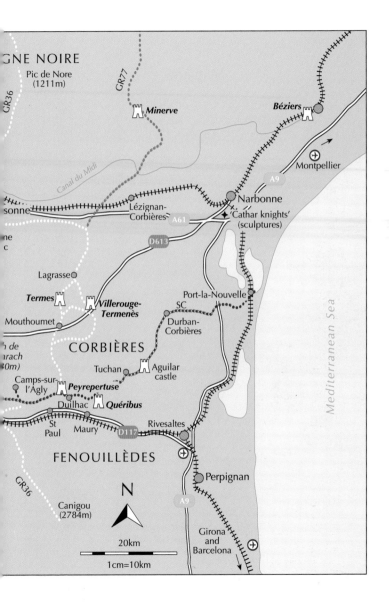

GNE NOIRE

Pic de Nore
(1211m)

GR77

GR36

Minerve

Béziers

Canal du Midi

Montpellier

A9

sonne

Lézignan-
Corbières

A61

Narbonne

'Cathar knights'
(sculptures)

D613

ne
c

Lagrasse

Port-la-Nouvelle

Termes

Villerouge-
Termenès

SC

Mouthoumet

Durban-
Corbières

h de
arach
0m)

CORBIÈRES

Tuchan

Aguilar
castle

Camps-sur-
l'Agly

Peyrepertuse

Duilhac

Quéribus

St
Paul

Maury

Rivesaltes

D117

FENOUILLÈDES

N

Canigou
(2784m)

GR36

Perpignan

20km

A9

1cm=10km

Girona
and
Barcelona

Mediterranean Sea

Map key

══════D117══════	principal road
══════A61══════	motorway
••••••••••••••••••••••	route (various colours)
························	other paths or tracks
– – – – – – – – – –	stream course (usually dry)
﹏﹏﹏﹏	river/stream or canal
┉┉┉┉┉┉┉┉┉	railway
◗	lake
⋒	Cathar castle
⬤	town/village
ⓒ	cave
⬆	hut (refuge)
⅄	pylon
■	isolated building or ruin
✳	notable viewpoint
P	car park
i	information office
⅄	campsite
▲	peak
❶	numbered point, referred to in text
○	tennis court
✦	monument, archaeological site or man-made feature of special interest

Map key

.	spot height
♦	church/chapel
⊞	cemetery
†	wayside cross
⊕	airport
⎵⎵⎵	ski tow
← ← ← ←	power line
⊓⊓⊓⊓⊓⊓	crags

Contour key

	2200-2400m
	2000-2200m
	1800-2000m
	1600-1800m
	1400-1600m
	1200-1400m
	1000-1200m
	800-1000m
	600-800m
	400-600m
	200-400m
	0-200m

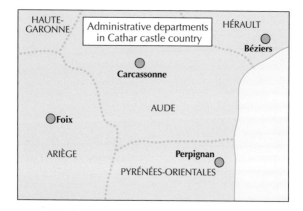

HAUTE-GARONNE

Administrative departments in Cathar castle country

HÉRAULT

Béziers

Carcassonne

AUDE

Foix

ARIÈGE

Perpignan

PYRÉNÉES-ORIENTALES

Walkers near Quéribus castle (Section 12)

PREFACE

The Cathars were a dissident sect of medieval Christians. They enjoyed widespread support in what is today southern France. In the 13th century they were brutally suppressed and took refuge in hilltop fortresses, known today as 'Cathar castles'.

Those castles are set in an area of beautiful countryside which offers excellent walking opportunities. It is a varied, challenging and fascinating region, enjoying plenty of sunshine and rich in wildlife. It has plentiful reasonably priced accommodation and abundant opportunities for wine tasting and gastronomic delectation.

The region is today one of France's most popular walking areas, but it was not always so – most of the walking routes in Cathar castle country seem to have been developed in relatively recent times. For example, when the traveller and author Nicholas Crane passed through St-Paul-de-Fenouillet in the early 1990s on his epic mountain walk across Europe, he was told that he was in the 'dead zone', where tourists were rarely seen, even in high summer. Today St-Paul is close to new waymarked walking routes, which pass beneath Quéribus and other Cathar castles. It is now frequented by walkers and visitors from many parts of Europe and beyond.

It seems that everyone who tours this stunning countryside and reads about the tragedy of the Cathars is moved by the landscape and by that story. Many are also gripped by the several legends that surround the Cathar castles – of buried treasure, the Holy Grail, sun worship, and contemplative ladies dressed in white who had an unfortunate knack of precipitating disaster.

This book concentrates mainly on the walks, the landscape, and the history of the Cathars' downfall. But, insofar as any lesson is drawn from this tour of a region that witnessed the crusade against the Cathars (and which, like most of Europe, also suffered two millennia of almost constant combat), that lesson is touched upon lightly in the final chapter. Entirely devoid of originality, that conclusion is at least brief. It is – quite simply – give peace a chance.

For that reason (among many others), this book is dedicated with gratitude to two lifelong campaigners for peace of my close acquaintance, namely my parents Pat and Alec Mattingly.

Alan Mattingly, Vernet-les-Bains

Like many Cathar castles, Lordat castle towers above its village (Section 6)

INTRODUCTION

This castle hath a pleasant seat; the air
Nimbly and sweetly recommends itself
Unto our gentle senses.
Macbeth, Act I

There is a point on a walk in this book where, after an hour or so's steady walking uphill on a track which winds through fields and woods rich in wild flowers and fungi, you emerge into a large clearing on high ground.

Imagine that you are standing there now. To the north, the ground falls and rises in a series of valleys and ridges. It is a warm, sleepy, thickly wooded landscape, rural France at its most rural. These are the foothills of the eastern Pyrenees. They ripple northwestwards towards the cathedral city of Toulouse and north-eastwards to the medieval spires of Carcassonne. At their far eastern end they meet the coastline of *la grande bleue*, the Mediterranean Sea.

In places, movements in the earth's crust in recent geological times thrust skywards immense slices of these foothills. Later, powerful torrents, fed by melting ice during colder millennia, sculpted from these blocks steep-sided peaks and razor-edge ridges. Much later, human beings seeking protection from their neighbours, bandits and invaders built fortified settlements on many of the high, isolated locations which

natural processes bequeathed to this region. Their owners constantly restored and strengthened those fortresses.

By the early medieval period this region was known as Languedoc. It was divided into a large number of near-independent baronies whose lords each possessed one or more castles. Many of those fortresses are today celebrated throughout the world as 'Cathar castles'. From your imaginary position, you are about to understand why the castles have achieved such fame.

Over your right shoulder, the ground rises again, to a hill covered in beech forest. Your footpath curves in the direction of that hill, and as you turn to cast your eye along its route, you may see white mist rushing up the left-hand side of the hill from far below. If the mist then starts to clear, be prepared for your jaw to drop. For what will emerge from the cloud, just beyond the beech-covered hill, is the sight of one of the most awesome and evocative rock pinnacles in Europe. There, soaring into the sky like a gigantic upright megalith, its craggy limestone slopes gleaming white, looms the 1200m Pog de Montségur (*pog* comes from the Occitan language, and means hill or mountain – see Montségur, section 9). On the very summit of the *pog* sit the formidable remains of the most renowned fortress in Cathar castle country.

It was here in 1244, after a siege lasting several months, that the principal mountain stronghold of the 'heretical' Languedoc Cathars fell. It was taken by the far superior forces of the French Crown and the Catholic Church. Shortly afterwards, 200 Cathars were burnt alive at the foot of the mountain.

WHO WERE THE CATHARS?

The term 'Cathar' was not used by the followers of this faith – who referred

Monument to the Cathars who were burnt at the stake below Montségur castle, 16 March 1244 (Section 9)

to themselves simply as Christians – but was employed by the Catholics when labelling this particular group of heretics. It may originally have been a term of offence, meaning cat-lover – that is, a sorcerer or witch. The Cathars' 'priests' – women as well as men – were referred to by their Catholic opponents as 'Perfects', meaning perfect (that is, complete) heretics. But they were known by their followers as simply good Christians, or *Bons Hommes* and *Bonnes Femmes*.

However, they had profound theological differences with the Catholic Church. In particular, they had a belief – dualism – that good and evil spring from different sources. Therefore the material world – which they saw as plainly evil – could not have been created by the God of the Bible. Such a belief was totally at odds with Catholic doctrine. The Cathars even saw the Catholic Church itself as the work of the devil. The broadcasting of such opinion was not a good strategy for surviving the heretic-burning years of medieval Europe.

The Cathar faith took root in Languedoc in the 11th century. The *Bons Hommes* and *Bonnes Femmes* who preached it were ascetic; they worked in the community as, for example, craftsmen; they preached in a language that everyone could understand; and they levied no taxes. Not surprisingly, their popularity spread rapidly among the independent-minded people of

Languedoc. The region's 'nobility' (its warlords) protected them; indeed, many members of 'noble' families in Languedoc were themselves Cathars.

From the outset, the Catholic Church saw the Cathars as a threat to its very existence. The French Crown, whose territory at that time was confined to the northern part of what is now France, became eager to take possession of Languedoc. These two irresistible forces, Church and Crown, together met head-on the immovable object of the Cathar faith. They launched against the Cathars a crusade just as cruel and bloody as those dispatched to 'save' the Holy Land. After a long struggle, the Cathar church was exterminated and the French Crown seized Languedoc.

After the crusade, the border of France moved south to Cathar country. It needed strong fortification against France's Spanish neighbours, so the French rebuilt and strengthened several of the castles in which the Cathars had once taken refuge. In the 17th century the border moved south once again, after a war that ended in triumph for the French. That left many of the 'Cathar castles' a long way north of the new border. The castles thus lost their strategic importance; most were demolished or abandoned, and then fell into ruin.

And thus the 'castles in the sky', now symbols of the Cathar faith and its demise, were bequeathed to posterity. The sometimes romantic, sometimes forbidding castles such as Montségur, Quéribus, Puilaurens, Peyrepertuse and Lastours became the centrepieces of fantastic fables and, in our time, tourist attractions of international repute.

The citadels we see today would have mostly been unrecognisable to the Cathars; in the majority of cases, the remains are of structures that were built after the Cathar period. But no matter: what is beyond dispute is that the castles offer stunning sights and are fascinating places to visit. They are irresistible focal points for fine walks in a lovely part of the French countryside. They will also forever be linked to the thought-provoking story of the Cathars, which touches everyone who visits this region.

Walking and thinking go together. Cathar castle country offers profound opportunities for both.

LANGUEDOC, THE 'CATHAR CASTLES' AND THE PAYS CATHARE

In medieval times, Languedoc was a large region in what is today south-central France. Its name was derived from the language spoken by its inhabitants (the *langue d'oc* – see below). The region was not a single administrative unit; its unity was based principally upon its language. The main city was Toulouse, in the west. Languedoc extended north towards the Dordogne, east towards the Rhône valley and south towards the Pyrenees.

Languedoc was invaded and occupied successively by the Romans, the Visigoths, the Moors and the Franks. In the 10th century it was divided up into feudal principalities, the biggest of which was the domain of the Count of Toulouse. Those principalities were not part of the French kingdom.

The Cathars propagated their beliefs in Languedoc from around the 11th century. In the middle of the 13th century, following the crusade that was launched to crush them, Languedoc became part of the French kingdom.

Today, the name 'Languedoc' survives in the title of the administrative region known as Languedoc-Roussillon, covering the administrative departments of Aude, Gard, Hérault, Lozère and the Pyrénées-Orientales. But medieval Languedoc was much bigger than today's Languedoc-Roussillon region.

The *langue d'oc* was a collection of Roman dialectics spoken in much of what is now southern France. It is in contrast to the *langue d'oïl*, the collection of Roman dialects which was spoken in the northern half of France and which formed the basis of the French language. The term *langue d'oc* is synonymous with 'Occitan'. It was a major language of culture in the Middle Ages and is still spoken today. Occitan is also used as an adjective, meaning of or from the area where the Occitan language is spoken.

The so-called Cathar castles are the medieval fortifications (or, more often, just the remains) that are found in Languedoc and located in places where the Cathars lived, preached or sought refuge. Many were built on vertiginous cliffs, crags or steep-sided pinnacles. They are striking in appearance and are loaded with sombre history and mystery. Today, these castles attract pilgrims, tourists, historians, archaeologists, writers, painters, treasure-hunters and charlatans with one of the most powerful magnetic forces of its kind in Europe.

Many of the castles were substantially reconstructed *after* the time of the Cathars. Little is known about how most of them looked when the Cathars inhabited them. However, they are located on sites with strong historical connections with the Cathars. 'Cathar castles' is a therefore a perfectly acceptable title.

A little information about each of the castles is given in the walk descriptions. The emphasis here is on walking rather than monuments, so this book does not offer detailed accounts of history, archaeology and legends. Plenty of literature covers those topics, much of it in English; books, leaflets and other publications are offered for sale at many of the castles, and in shops and information centres round about (see Appendix 2).

An entrance fee is charged for access to most of the Cathar castles featured in this book. Subsequent chapters give general indications of

Looking down on Foix from a viewpoint on the Foix walks (Section 4)

the times of the year when these are open to the public. Detailed information about current opening times can be obtained from local tourist infor-mation offices (see walk descriptions and Appendix 1). If you plan to visit several castles and other monuments in the area it is worth buying a *carte inter-sites*, which gives a discounted entrance fee to 16 places.

Bear in mind that some castles merit a long visit; you could spend half a day exploring the nooks and crannies of the extensive remains of Peyrepertuse. At the other end of the spectrum, there is very little left of the castles at Montaillou and Minerve. However, the latter are worth seeing, as they provide a tangible link to poignant historical events.

Anyone who visits the area will see *Pays Cathare* ('Cathar country') signs along the way. The French department of Aude, centred on Carcassonne, refers to itself as the *Pays Cathare*. However, this name is used by public and commercial organisations over a much wider area than that covered by Aude alone.

The Sentier Cathare long-distance footpath runs east–west across Cathar castle country, from Port-la-Nouvelle on the coast to Foix. It is a popular route, and sections of it are incorporated in some of the walks in this book. The Aude department's *Pays Cathare* logo appears on signposts along much of the Sentier Cathare.

That logo is used widely throughout Cathar castle country. It is a curious emblem which apparently depicts the sun (or maybe the moon) rising above the land. In doing so it represents the influence that the Cathar religion radiated over this country. The sun/moon is divided into a black sector and a white sector,

representing the dualism of the Cathar faith. The slightly scribbled appearance of the motif is said to denote the 'cuts' that were inflicted on this region by the painful events of the crusade against the Cathars.

Subtle the *Pays Cathare* logo may be, but the extent to which the Cathar theme is exploited to attract tourists is the antithesis of subtlety. Signs and advertisements for enterprises with names like 'Cathar-ama', 'le relais Cathare', 'Cathare Immobilier' (an estate agent) proliferate. A 20th-century motorway (the A61 west of Narbonne) has been named 'le chemin des Cathares', and a sign at an exit from the A9 coastal motorway even offers you a welcome to 'the beaches of the Pays Cathare'.

The Pays Cathare *logo seen here on an information board near Quéribus castle*

'CATHAR CASTLE COUNTRY'

This term has been coined simply for the purposes of this book, and the area so defined lies in a part of Languedoc that is southeast of Toulouse. Béziers is in the northeast corner; the Mediterranean forms its eastern border; the southern border is a line running roughly between Perpignan and Ax-les-Thermes; and the Ariège valley, which runs through Foix, forms the western border (see map on page 6–7). Most of the best-known Cathar castles are found within Cathar castle country.

However, it should be remembered that the Cathars were based over a much wider area than that defined as 'Cathar castle country'. The Cathars' main centre was Toulouse; their influence extended far to the north of Carcassonne, to Albi and beyond. The name often given to the crusade launched against the Cathars – the Albigensian crusade – is derived from the Cathars' association with Albi. The Cathars were also numerous in other parts of western Europe, including northern Italy and the Rhineland; but in all these places they were sooner or later ruthlessly crushed by their enemies.

When you are in the country of the Cathars, you can count on being frequently reminded of your whereabouts.

GETTING THERE

It is possible to reach Cathar country by plane and/or train from many parts of Britain in a day.

By air

There are major international airports at Toulouse, Montpellier, Marseille and Barcelona with direct scheduled flights from a number of places in Britain (for example, at the time of writing Easyjet has flights from several British destinations to Barcelona, and from London to Toulouse and Marseille). From each of those airports there are rail connections and motorways giving relatively

fast connections to, for example, Carcassonne, Béziers and Perpignan. Rail and road connections from Toulouse south to Foix are also good.

Ryanair has flights from London to Carcassonne, Montpellier, Nîmes (not far from Montpellier) and Perpignan; from Liverpool to Nimes; and from several British cities to Girona. (Girona airport is northeast of Barcelona, and gives easier access than Barcelona airport if you are then driving north to France). Flybe has flights from Birmingham, Southampton and Bristol to Toulouse and, in the summer, from Birmingham and Southampton to Perpignan.

By rail

If you travel all the way from Britain by train, via Eurostar's Channel Tunnel service to, say, Béziers, try to change

19

The 'Cathar knights' – huge modern sculptures by Jacques Tissinier – overlook the A61 motorway near Narbonne. The knights greet many visitors who travel from the north to Cathar castle country.

trains in Lille rather than Paris. That way you only have to cross to another platform, not to the other side of a city.

By road

You can get to Cathar castle country by coach, but London–Perpignan takes around 24hr. For information contact Eurolines (tel: 08705 143219; **www.nationalexpress.com**).

If you travel by road, you can cross France on autoroutes (motorways) all the way – bear in mind that these are toll roads. They can be extremely busy in school holiday periods, especially in July and August. There are often long hold-ups in high summer on the A7 autoroute between Lyon and Orange, which funnels holiday traffic down the Rhône valley.

General travel information

Information can be obtained from: French Travel Centre (see Appendix 1); French Railways (tel: 0870

8306030; **www.raileurope.co.uk**); British Airways (tel: 0870 850 9850 within UK; tel: 08 25 82 50 40 within France; **www.britishairways.com**) and Ryanair (tel: 0871 246 0000 within UK; tel: 08 92 55 56 66 within France; **www.ryanair.com**).

For SNCF, the national French railway service, contact **www.sncf.com**. It has an English version and gives times and prices of rail services in France.

The Thomas Cook European Timetable for trains across Europe is worth consulting if much of your travelling to and around Cathar castle country is by rail. A new edition is published every month, and it is widely available in British bookshops for around £10.

GETTING AROUND

Main roads and railway lines within Cathar castle country are shown on the location map (see page 6–7). There are two main east–west transport axes:

- Narbonne–Carcassonne–Toulouse corridor, followed by the A61 autoroute and by good rail and bus services.
- Perpignan–Quillan–Foix corridor, followed by a main road, the D117 (single carriageway for most of the way). Bus services run along this corridor, but they are infrequent (more frequent at the eastern end). A summer tourist train service, the Train du Pays Cathare et du Fenouillèdes, operates between Rivesaltes (north of Perpignan) and Axat (just south of Quillan) – see **http://perso.wanadoo.fr/tpcf**.

There are three main north–south transport axes:

- Béziers–Narbonne–Perpignan corridor, parallel and close to the Mediterranean coastline; followed by the A9 autoroute and good rail and bus services
- Carcassonne–Quillan corridor, along the Aude valley. This is also followed by a main road, the D118 (single carriageway for much of the way). There are reasonably good rail and bus services between Carcassonne and Quillan
- Toulouse–Foix–Ax-les-Thermes corridor, along the Ariège valley. The main road through this corridor is the N20 (partly double

The Bassin des Ladres in the centre of Ax-les-Thermes – a good base for exploring much of Cathar castle country. (The pool is fed by a hot spring and has been here since the time of the Cathars; sore feet love it.)

and partly single carriageway). There are good rail and bus services along the corridor.

Elsewhere public transport services are scarce. Buses serve several towns and villages away from these main transport corridors, but these are often mainly designed to get children to and from school. They are therefore infrequent and may not run during the school holidays.

Other roads, of intermediate and minor status, wind across the hills and valleys and carry relatively little traffic. They can be pleasant to drive or cycle along if you are not in a hurry, but you do have to be constantly on the alert for fast-moving vehicles that may suddenly come hurtling towards you around the bend just ahead.

ACCOMMODATION

Places to stay are plentiful, from simple campsites to swanky hotels. Some advice is given later in this section about how to locate and reserve the sort of accommodation that you want. If in doubt, good starting points for making enquiries and seeking relevant literature are the French Travel Centre in London or a relevant tourist information office in Cathar castle country (see Appendix 1). Many bookshops in Britain also sell guides to accommodation in France.

Most hotels, *gîtes*, campsites, and so on are open from Easter to October. Many, especially those in or near cities and large towns, are open for all or most of the year. It is highly desirable to check room/bed availability in advance and to reserve accommodation. This is especially so for July and August, when many establishments are fully booked, and for those places near the coast or in internationally renowned tourist sites like Carcassonne. In addition, several establishments in the countryside are closed for all or most of the winter months.

Many establishments, in all price ranges, have not only e-mail addresses, but also websites giving information about their facilities and inviting you to book accommodation online. It will soon be the norm for accommodation providers to offer an online booking facility.

Gîtes d'étape are rather like youth hostels. They are reasonably priced and most towns and sizeable villages have at least one. Many are run as private enterprises, but often they are managed by the local *commune*. Like youth hostels, they vary a good deal in size, comfort and facilities. You can't always count on getting meals, but there is usually a café, restaurant or grocer's nearby. See **www.gite-etape.com**. The website **www.gites-refuges.com** is another useful source of information about *gîtes* and other types of simple accommodation.

There are four youth hostels in the area: Carcassonne, Bugarach, Quillan and Perpignan. The French

Youth Hostels association is at 9 rue de Brantome, 75003 Paris; tel: (00 33) (0)1 48 04 70 30; **www.fuaj.org**.

Gîtes rurals are self-catering houses, cottages or apartments in the countryside or along the coast. These too vary considerably in size and facilities, but quality is generally good and they can offer excellent value for families or small groups who want to establish a base for a week or two and go out on day excursions. You can get particularly good bargains if you book out of the main holiday periods. Contact Gîtes de France: La Maison des Gîtes de France et du Tourisme Vert, 59 rue Saint-Lazare, 75439 Paris Cedex 09; tel: (00 33) (0)1 49 70 75 75; **www.gites-de-france.fr**.

There are plentiful *chambres d'hôtes*, the French equivalent of bed and breakfast establishments (indeed, an increasing number are advertising themselves as 'bed and breakfast'). Gîtes de France also promotes *chambres d'hôtes* and is a good source of information. *Bed & Breakfast in France 2004* (£12.99) is a co-publication by the AA and the French Gîtes de France which lists over 3000 bed and breakfast establishments around France.

Hotels are not quite so abundant, but you won't have any trouble finding one if you stay in towns like Carcassonne and Quillan, or head for large villages like Montségur and Cucugnan which are close to the best-known Cathar castles. Hotels which bear the *Logis de France* label seem to be invariably reliable and good value. The *Logis de France* guidebook to its recommended hotels is sold in some bookshops in Britain and France and is worth buying; for central reservations tel: (00 33) (0)1 45 84 83 84; see also **www.logis-de-fr.fr**. The famous Michelin red guide to hotels in France can also be invaluable. Lists of hotels in and near particular towns can be looked up on **www.viamichelin.com**.

Auberge is a term adopted by a wide variety of establishments. Some are *gîtes d'étape*, others are hotels. What they generally have in common is that there is a restaurant of some sort on the premises.

Campsites abound; for information see **www.campingfrance.com**.

STOCKING UP

There are many towns and large villages along the main transport corridors where you can count on finding at least one store, like a supermarket or *épicerie* (grocer's-cum-general store), open on most days throughout the year. Bear in mind that, like almost everything else in France (apart from restaurants), they will probably be closed for two or three hours from midday. Most such places also have a chemist (*pharmacie* – look out for a flashing green cross), a *boulangerie* (bakery) and other shops.

Banks and post offices are more widely spaced out. The opening hours

Stock up when you can. Several farms along the way sell excellent produce, as here on the Pech de Bugarach walk (Section 16).

of many banks may be restricted (for example, mornings only). If you can't find a post office and you only want a few stamps, try a tobacconist – they usually sell them.

Distances between petrol stations can be quite considerable, even along the main transport corridors. When they are not staffed, some operate automatically with credit card machines – but the machines may accept only French credit cards. Remember too that some of the simpler accommodation establishments will not accept payment by credit card. That can also be the case in many small shops, bars and restaurants that will only accept payment by French cheque or cash.

Away from the main transport corridors, many villages are now without permanent shops, bakery and

even bars. Some have such facilities, but they are only open in the peak holiday periods. Local residents may rely upon 'travelling shops' – vans and lorries loaded with food and everyday items, which tour villages, acting as a mobile *épiceries*.

Along long-distance paths and other well-used walking routes, farms will often sell cheese, milk, honey, fruit and so on to passers-by.

It's a good idea to keep well stocked-up with essential foodstuffs (if you are on a cross-country trek), with petrol (if you are motoring), and with cash – however you choose to travel.

MAPS

The sketch maps accompanying the walk descriptions in this book are intended only to offer an indication of the key features in the areas crossed. It is strongly recommended that walkers also equip themselves with the relevant 1:25,000 maps published by the Institut Géographique National (IGN), the French equivalent of the Ordnance Survey in Britain. These excellent maps contain very detailed topographical information. Each walk description specifies the 1:25,000 map (or maps) which cover the relevant area.

There are two types of 1:25,000 map. Maps in the *Serie Bleue* series each cover an area of about 15km x 20km. Maps in the *Cartes topographiques TOP 25* series vary in

Always keep a map in your pack (seen here below Puilaurens castle, Section 11)

size but typically cover an area of about 27km x 22km.

The *TOP 25* maps show long-distance paths, local walking routes and a lot of other valuable tourist information, much of which is not shown on the *Serie Bleue* maps. They cover coastal, mountain and other tourist areas. In Cathar castle country, most of the 1:25,000 maps are in the *TOP 25* series.

A grid of numbered kilometre squares covers the maps of newer editions of both 1:25,000 series. The newer editions can also be used with global positioning devices (a GPS symbol is shown on the front). At the time of writing, about two-thirds of the 1:25,000 maps referred to in this book are GPS-compatible. The newer editions of all 1:25,000 maps are also being marketed as *Cartes de randonnée* (walkers' maps).

Many newsagents, bookshops and supermarkets in France sell IGN

maps. *TOP 25* maps cost around 10 Euros each (about £7), while a *Serie Bleue* map costs around 8 Euros.

The publisher Rando éditions has produced a series of 1:50,000 maps covering the French Pyrenees and their northern foothills, using IGN cartography and also called *Cartes de randonnées*. In this series, no 9, Montségur, covers an area between Quillan and Foix and is useful for planning walks in the area. It costs around 10 Euros.

The IGN also produces a series of 1:50,000 maps, but these are not usually available in shops and, for walkers, are no adequate substitute for 1:25,000 maps.

For route-planning purposes the IGN's series of 1:100,000 maps (the *Cartes topographiques Top 100* series, or *Cartes de promenade*) is very helpful. Nos 71 (St-Gaudens Andorre) and 72 (Béziers Perpignan) cover most of Cathar castle country.

IGN's 1:250,000 maps (*Cartes régionales* series) are also designed for route planning by road. Cathar castle country is covered by *Midi-Pyrénées* (R16) and *Languedoc-Roussillon* (R17). In France, the 1:100,000 and 1:250,000 maps currently cost around 5 Euros each.

IGN's website is **www.ign.fr** (in French only). Their maps and other products can be bought via that website using a British credit card. But, with the additional postage and cost of currency transfer, their final prices seem to work out a little higher than those charged by British suppliers of the same maps.

WEATHER, EQUIPMENT, RISKS

On the whole, the weather in Cathar castle country is very agreeable. Nevertheless – although the Mediterranean is not far away – don't imagine that this region is similar to torrid Andalusia or bone-dry Crete. Rather, the weather is like that of Kent – only more so. Winter days are often cold and blustery, but springtime starts earlier and the summers are hotter and last longer. There are more sunny days throughout the year.

However, the climate has a great capacity to catch you out. A hot day in summer can start sunny and clear but a tremendous thunderstorm can suddenly build up in the early afternoon. Typically, that storm could – but not always – vent its fury in less than 30min. In winter there might be weeks of mild, dry weather followed by a day in which half a metre of snow is suddenly dumped on higher ground.

The occasional fierce and unrelenting winds may also surprise. One such wind is the *tramontane*, which comes from the northwest. Its often-cold temperature can be guarded against with adequate warm clothing and, insofar as it may blow away the

Weather: usually sunny and warm, but be ready for occasional surprises (this was the summit of the Pech de Bugarach on an abnormal day in mid-April)

clouds and let the sun shine through, it can be welcome. But take great care if you are walking on a hill or mountain ridge when the *tramontane* is at full blast.

The climate also varies a great deal from east to west. On any given day, the weather in the east may be hot and dry, while in the west conditions could be cooler with occasional showers. The vegetation shows corresponding differences. For example, in the east you will find dry, open plateaux covered in *garrigue* vegetation – scented, often spiky Mediterranean shrubs and herbs. By

You will often see lines of wind turbines stretched out across high plateaux, now almost as characteristic of Cathar castle country as the castles themselves. None of the walks in this book passes beneath or very close to these.

contrast, in the west there is much humid deciduous forest, where beech trees grow to regal proportions.

Less surprisingly, the climate also changes with altitude. The walks in this book vary from a canal towpath walk at near sea level to a rugged mountain hike at an altitude of over 2300m. For the former, light clothing and trainers will be perfectly adequate, even on some winter days. For the latter you should wear walking boots and carry adequate warm and waterproof clothing at all times of the year.

It is difficult to generalise about the sort of clothing and equipment that you should take with you on these walks. If, for example, you are planning to walk between Easter and early autumn, and undertaking a wide range of walks (including the mountain routes), bring the same range of clothing and equipment that you would pack for, say, a summer walking tour of any upland range in England. Make sure that includes light clothing (T-shirts and shorts) because – if you are lucky with the weather – you may find that you wear little else.

If you already have some experience of walking in various types of terrain in Britain, you won't need to be told that you should always carry a good map and a compass, especially if going into the hills. **Make sure you are equipped with the relevant map(s) and carry a compass – and are capable of using it – when**

attempting any of the walks described in this book. If you have not done much upland walking before coming to Cathar castle country, read up about it beforehand – get hold of a copy of Cicerone's *The Hillwalker's Manual* by Bill Birkett.

Two things, however, do need to be stressed.

• On a day's walk in this region, at any time of the year, you will almost certainly build up much more of a thirst than you would when walking in Britain. Drinking water is sometimes available at natural springs or drinking taps. But it is best to assume that you will not come across any, so always carry plenty of drinking water with you.

• Carry (and apply liberally!) effective sun lotion. In that respect this region does bear comparison with Andalusia and Crete.

A few other warnings are called for (see below), but don't let these deter you from visiting Cathar castle country. It is, on the whole, a pretty safe place.

The sudden storms mentioned above can cause rivers to rise with amazing rapidity; dry streambeds can become raging torrents with a matter of hours. If your walk includes a stretch of dry riverbed, or a key river crossing, be aware that those sections may become impassable after very heavy rainfall. In the walk descriptions advice is given about possible options.

The storms may be accompanied by lightning. If you can shelter in a mountain refuge (or an *orri*, an old drystone shepherd's hut) while a storm rages, well and good. But the likelihood is that the storm will break before you can reach one. Sit on your rucksack in open ground after laying aside anything metal (such as walking poles). You will get very wet, but you will minimise the risk of being struck by lightning. You should dry out quickly in the sun once the storm has passed.

Lightning may also cause fire. Fortunately, this part of France suffers much less from fires in forest and undergrowth than does hotter, drier Provence, further east. If you find yourself anywhere near an uncontrolled fire, get away from it as quickly as possible. Flames can move across the ground with startling speed, especially when fanned by a strong wind. Needless to say, walkers should take great care not to start a fire themselves.

If you are walking anywhere in this region from September to February, don't be surprised to hear the occasional sharp crack of gunfire, probably from hunters tracking down wild boar or, on the higher ground, deer. You may also see signs alongside footpaths warning you that shooting is taking place in the area. It is very unlikely that you will be shot; the hunters

Look out for...

Snakes are rarely sighted, and the majority are not poisonous. Perhaps the most 'dangerous' creature that you are likely to encounter is – surprisingly – a caterpillar. In the early spring, especially beneath or near pine trees, you may see curious, worm-like lines of hairy brown caterpillars winding across the ground. These are processional caterpillars, that overwinter in a cotton-wool cocoon high up in a pine tree. They chomp on the pine leaves and can leave whole forests devastated. In spring they come down to earth, form head-to-tail chains and wander around looking for somewhere to bury themselves. Don't touch them or get too close – they have a nasty sting. Above all, keep your dog well away, or you could be facing a distressing trip to the nearest vet.

Processional caterpillars: possibly the region's most dangerous creatures

have to comply with strict safety regulations, including not firing across footpaths. Stick carefully to the waymarked path and offer a cheerful *bonjour* as you go past.

You have even less cause for concern if you ever actually see a wild boar. The sight of anything resembling *Homo sapiens* will cause it to turn on its heels and dash off without a second's hesitation. Wolves and bears live in Cathar castle country, but in extremely small numbers. They do eat sheep and other livestock for breakfast (in 2004 a bear polished off a couple of pigs in Niort, just south of Quillan, before being chased away), but your chances of meeting one of these creatures is infinitely small.

Pyrenean sheep dogs – big, beautiful, white-haired creatures – are often employed by farmers to guard flocks of sheep and goats while they graze. These dogs are usually unaccompanied by shepherds. They may utter a few warning barks in your direction, but present no danger to walkers. If you have a dog with you, keep it well under control (as in all circumstances). Pyrenean sheep dogs are trained to issue summary justice to bears, wolves and stray dogs which threaten their flock, so don't give them reason to take issue with your pet.

Sheep and cattle are often fenced in. Even high up on open country you will come across wire fences. They rarely present an insuperable barrier, but always be careful how you cross them; they might be electrified. Some

electric fences are powered by solar panels.

As caterpillars descend, plants shoot up. In spring and early summer undergrowth can rapidly become exceptionally dense, especially in the western part of the area. The paths followed on the walks described all seem popular, so the passage of walkers should keep most of them clear. But one or two sections were overgrown when the walks were surveyed. Where this may be a problem a suggested alternative route is given.

Finally, take a note of emergency telephone numbers, posted up in information offices, gîtes, hotels, and so on. If you ever need to telephone for help or to report an accident or a fire and are not sure who best to call, ring 18 (the French fire service, the *sapeurs pompiers*, which deals with many types of emergency). However, bear in mind that mobile telephones will not always work in remoter areas of countryside. Always ensure that you have adequate insurance in case you have to be rescued or need emergency medical treatment.

WAYMARKED WALKING ROUTES

In Cathar castle country, where green tourism is flourishing, most *communes* (roughly equivalent to parish councils) have one or more waymarked walks in their territory. Often a notice board in the square of the main village will display these, and publications describing them may be available from the local tourist office or town hall (*mairie*).

It is becoming common practice for adjacent *communes* to band together as *communautés de communes*. Those joint organisations often take responsibility for planning, waymarking and publicising local walking circuits in the area they cover. An example in Cathar castle country is the Communauté de Communes Pays d'Olmes, based in the town of Lavelanet, east of Foix. It has developed a fine network of local waymarked circuits. Sections of those circuits have been incorporated in walks described in the Roquefixade and Montségur sections of this book. Later sections and Appendix 2 contain information about relevant publications covering local walks.

The Fédération Française de la Randonnée Pédestre (FFRP) has also published several *Topo-guides* for local walks (**www.ffrp.asso.fr**). These are for PR paths, *Promenades Randonnées*, which roughly means walks that can be completed in a day or less. Like the FFRP's series of *Topo-guides* for GR (*Grande Randonnée*) long-distance paths, the PR *Topo-guides* have a uniform format. The maps, illustrations, route descriptions and complementary information are of a high quality.

Relevant PR *Topo-guides* are referred to in Appendix 2 and in various walk descriptions. The local walks described in these guidebooks

Local walking circuits are usually waymarked in yellow – as on this sign-post above Montségur (Section 9)

are waymarked with painted yellow rectangles. Most other local walking circuits in Cathar castle country are also now indicated by yellow waymarks (but not always: for instance, a section of the hill walk described in the Montaillou section is indicated by red waymarks).

GR paths carry red and white waymarks. A few – the GR7, GR36 and GR77 – cross Cathar castle country. Regional GRP (*Grande Randonnée de Pays*) paths carry red and yellow waymarks. There are a few of those in the area too, such as the *Tours du Pays d'Olmes*, near Roquefixade. The Sentier Cathare carries red and yellow waymarks for

31

much of its route in Ariège, but blue and yellow waymarks in Aude.

It should be noted that where a section of a local walking route (normally indicated by yellow waymarks) coincides with the route of a GR or GRP path, the waymarks of the latter may take priority. The GR/GRP waymarks may thus be the only waymarks along that section of the local circuit.

For each walk there are notes on what kinds of waymarks to look out for, and (where appropriate) on which ones to ignore. For example, you may see waymarks consisting of a triangle and two adjacent discs, indicating the routes of mountain bike circuits. For the most part, they are best ignored.

Local walking circuits are susceptible to modification at any time. Please bear in mind that the routes of some of the walks described may be amended in the future. If in doubt, follow the routes indicated by any new waymarking on the ground.

THE WALKS DESCRIBED IN THIS BOOK

The 16 walk sections describe several walks in Cathar castle country. All the walks follow waymarked and well-maintained routes. They can all be accomplished in a day or less. Several of the walks are circular; some are out-and-back walks, which return to the starting point by the outward route. A couple follow figure-of-eight circuits; one is a linear walk.

Each of the walk sections describes one or two walks. In a few cases, a variant of a walk is also suggested, giving the option of lengthening or shortening that particular walk.

Walks from other books and guides have not been simply copied (although the author is grateful to the French authors of other publications for the ideas and inspiration that they provided). Sometimes a section of one local walking circuit has, for example, been joined with a section of another. Elsewhere, a section of a long-distance path has been combined with part of a local circuit. All the walks have been selected for their quality and interest, for the absence of significant problems in following them on the ground, and have been carefully checked.

The waymarking varies from walk to walk. On the whole, the waymarking symbols used on the ground are self-explanatory. Simple rectangles or discs indicate that you should carry straight on. Symbols that bend or point to the right or left indicate that you are approaching a path turning. A cross usually indicates a route that you should not take.

The routes avoid road walking as much as possible. Where this is unavoidable, the roads concerned usually carry little motor traffic. But don't be lulled into a false sense of security by the apparent tranquillity of the route. Listen and look out for approaching vehicles.

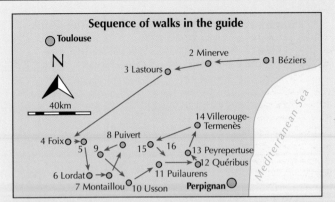

The focal points of the walks in this book are mostly Cathar castles. The walks are arranged in an order that roughly follows the chronological sequence of events that led to the crushing of the Cathars in Languedoc in the 13th century, as follows:

1 **Béziers** The crusade led by French forces against the Cathars of independent Languedoc began here in **July 1209**. The town was sacked and its inhabitants massacred.

2 **Minerve** The crusaders' army seized Carcassonne in **August 1209**, then besieged and captured Minerve castle in **1210**. The first mass execution of Cathars took place here.

3 **Lastours** The crusaders captured this key castle in **1211**.

4 **Foix** The crusaders' army won a decisive victory at the battle of Muret (near Toulouse) in **1213**. They then took Foix, another Cathar stronghold, in **1215**.

5 **Roquefixade** After a period in which the crusaders suffered setbacks, they returned with irresistible strength, led by the French king. The Treaty of Paris, signed in **April 1229**, led to Languedoc being absorbed into the French kingdom. Roquefixade lay in the heart of the hill country to which many Cathars thereafter retreated.

6 **Lordat** The castle was handed over by the Count of Foix in **June 1229**.

7 **Montaillou** The Inquisition was launched in **1233** to terrorise Cathar supporters. Its records describe in detail life in Montaillou, making it possibly the best-documented medieval village in Europe.

8 **Puivert** The castle was taken in 1210. The defeated lord's son took part in the **1242** massacre of Inquisition leaders in Avignonet.

9 **Montségur** This, the most famous Cathar stronghold, was besieged and taken in **March 1244**. Over 200 Cathars were burnt at the stake.

10 **Usson** Cathar escapees from Montségur, possibly carrying treasure, took refuge in this castle in **1244**.

11 **Puilaurens** A hideout for some post-Montségur Cathars after **1244**.

12 **Quéribus** Said to be the last of the Cathar strongholds, it was taken in **1255**.

13 **Peyrepertuse** Surrendered in 1240. After the Treaty of Corbeil **1258**, it became, like other Cathar castles, a fortress defending the French kingdom's new southern frontier.

14 **Villerouge-Termenès** The last Languedoc Cathar 'priest' (Bon Homme) was burnt at the stake here in **1321**.

15 **Rennes-le-Château** Site of a fable about Cathar treasure which begins in **1891**.

16 **Pech de Bugarach** One of the most striking summits in the area. From the top you can survey nearly all of Cathar castle country.

Summary of the Walks Described in this Book

Walk Sections	Walks in each Section	Character of Walk	Estimated Walking Time
1 Béziers	Main walk	Out-and-back canal towpath walk	6.5hr
	Shorter variant	Out-and-back canal towpath walk	3.5hr
2 Minerve	Long walk	Circular hill walk	5hr
	Short walk	Circular hill walk	2hr
3 Lastours	Long walk	Figure-of-eight hill walk	6hr
	Short walk	Circular hill walk	2hr
4 Foix	Long walk	Linear hill walk	5hr
	Short walk	Out-and-back hill walk	3hr
5 Roquefixade	Roquefixade walk	Circular hill walk	3hr
6 Lordat	Lordat castle walk	Circular hill walk	3hr
	Lordat mountain walk	Out-and-back mountain walk	5hr
7 Montaillou	Montaillou walk	Circular hill walk	6hr
8 Puivert	Walk north of Nébias	Circular hill and limestone labyrinth walk	3hr
	Walk south of Nébias	Circular hill walk	5hr
9 Montségur	Montségur castle walk	Circular hill walk	6hr
	Shorter variant	Out-and-back hill walk	3hr
	Montségur mountain walk	Circular mountain walk	7hr
10 Usson	Usson walk	Figure-of-eight hill walk	5.5hr
11 Puilaurens	Puilaurens walk	Circular forest/hill walk	3.5hr
	Variant with link from Lapradelle	Circular forest/hill walk	5.5hr
12 Quéribus	Long walk	Rugged out-and-back hill walk	6.5hr
	Shorter variant	Up by the long walk, down by a more direct return route with road walking	5.5hr
	Circular walk	Circular hill walk	3.5hr
13 Peyrepertuse	Long walk ('La Quille')	Out-and-back hill walk	5.5hr
	Longer variant	Out by the long walk, back by a longer hill route	6.5hr
	Short walk ('Moulin de Ribaute')	Circular hill walk with rock pools	2.5hr
14 Villerouge-Termenès	Serre de Blanes walk	Out-and-back hill walk	3hr
	GR36AB walk (Villerouge-Termenès castle to Termes castle)	Long out-and-back hill walk	6hr
15 Rennes-le-Château	Rennes-le-Château walk	Circular hill walk	4hr
16 The Pech de Bugarach	Scrambler's circuit	Rugged circular hill walk	6hr
	Popular promenade	Out-and-back hill walk	3.5hr

Each of the walk sections has a focal point. Most are Cathar castles, including the most renowned, such as Peyrepertuse and Quéribus. The walk (or walks) pass by, or are in sight of, the castle. In most cases there will be enough time to complete a walk and visit the castle on the same day. In a few cases it would be tiring and possibly impracticable to do, in which case you must save your castle visit for another day.

The order in which the walk sections are presented broadly follows an anticlockwise circuit around Cathar castle country (see page 33), beginning in Béziers (where the crusade against the Cathars began) and ending on the summit of the Pech de Bugarach. It is hoped that this sequence will

assist anyone who is touring the area. It also follows chronologically the story of how Catharism in Languedoc was crushed in the 13th and early 14th centuries. Each walk section contains a short commentary on the historical associations of the area with the Cathars.

HOW TO USE THIS GUIDE

At the start of each walk section there is a summary of the following walk (or walks) and the area's terrain. Next comes a look at relevant events in the Cathar story ('Cathar history') that relate to the focal point of the section – a Cathar castle or other location.

You will then find practical information relating to the walk(s), including:

Foix castle: a famous emblem of Cathar castle country, and the finishing point of the walks in Section 4

- How to get to the starting point(s)
- Points concerning navigation (with particular reference to waymarking).

A detailed route description of each walk then follows, starting with:
- Estimated distance, altitude, walking time and relevant maps (including any variant).

Following the route description are:
- A summary of any variant
- A box containing points of interest along or near the route, and advice on how much time to allow for visiting the castle and/or other nearby places of interest and where you can obtain further information.

Please note the following:
- Estimated visiting times, distances and altitudes are approximate (apart from a few specific spot heights).
- 'Time' is the estimated time spent while actually walking, including short breaks (for example, to take photographs and recover breath). It doesn't cover longer periods for lunch, an afternoon siesta, and so on. Figures are based on the pace of a moderately fit and experienced walker who is alone or in a small party.

- The description of the route contains bracketed numbers that correspond to numbered locations on the relevant sketch map.
- For the most part, the description concentrates on route directions. Points of interest are highlighted in **bold**, and covered in more detail at the end of each walk description.
- Sketch maps of the routes accompany the text.
- Where two walks are described, there are sometimes two separate sketch maps; in other cases, both walks are marked on the same sketch map (in different colours).
- Where a variant is described, only those sections that differ from the route of the main walk are shown on the sketch map.

Bonne promenade!

1 BÉZIERS

One walk – with a shorter variant – is suggested in this section. It is essentially a long, out-and-back route along the tree-lined towpath of the Canal du Midi, starting from Béziers railway station and leading to a famous pre-Roman hilltop archaeological site, the Oppidum d'Ensérune. En route, the charming canal-side village of Colombiers is passed. The surrounding landscape is Mediterranean lowland, mostly covered in vineyards. There is a 100m climb at the far end, but otherwise the route is level.

CATHAR HISTORY: JULY 1209

By the early part of the 13th century, the Cathar 'heresy' had many followers in Languedoc. Successive popes called upon Catholic nobles and kings to suppress the Cathar church and its followers – by force if necessary. As a reward, the 'crusaders' were offered the land and possessions of the Cathars and their supporters.

In 1208 the papal envoy Pierre de Castelnau was murdered near Saint-Gilles, south of Avignon. He had been pursuing a mission of persecution against the Cathars, and supporters of the latter were held responsible for his death. Pope Innocent III once again called for a military crusade against the Cathars. The French king responded by allowing several of his barons to form a huge army, which marched south down the Rhône valley towards Languedoc.

In July 1209 the French army arrived at the walls of Béziers. For the most part, the Catholic and Cathar inhabitants were united in their determination to repulse the invaders. The town walls were sound and the defenders well equipped, so initially it seemed as if the siege could last a long time. But a group of Béziers citizens opened an entrance to the town so as to launch a surprise attack on part of the French camp, and in their retreat did not have time to close the entrance securely. The French army took immediate advantage of this breach, and poured into the town with overwhelming force.

As the massacre and pillage got underway the pope's legate, Arnaud Amaury, was asked by French soldiers how they could distinguish Catholics from Cathars. Amaury's reputed reply was utterly cold-blooded, and established at the outset the crusade's brutal character. 'Kill them all,' he said, 'God will know his own.'

Thousands of people were slaughtered in Béziers on 22 July 1209. Even the cathedral was set alight so that those who sought sanctuary there – including many women and children – could not escape.

The first and only 'crusade' to be launched in a Christian land had begun with one of the most horrific events in French history.

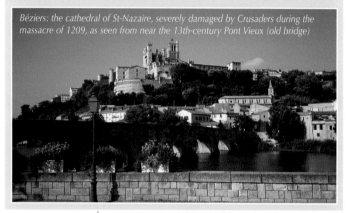

Béziers: the cathedral of St-Nazaire, severely damaged by Crusaders during the massacre of 1209, as seen from near the 13th-century Pont Vieux (old bridge)

PRACTICAL INFORMATION
Access to starting points
Béziers is served by several rail and bus services. It can be reached directly by rail from Paris. It is also close to the A9 motorway running parallel to the Mediterranean coastline.

Béziers town bus no 13 goes from the centre to the Ecluses de Fonseranes. It runs almost hourly on Sundays but is less frequent on other days of the week. There is a car park at the foot of the locks.

Navigation
There is no waymarking on this walk, but it is not necessary; navigation is ultra-easy.

ROUTE DESCRIPTION
(Numbers in the text refer to the sketch map.) With the entrance to **Béziers** railway station behind you (1), and

Distances:	main walk 25km (15.5 miles); variant 13km (8.1 miles)
Altitude:	near sea level to 130m
Time:	main walk 6.5hr; variant 3.5hr
Map:	IGN 1:25,000 2545ET (Béziers); Béziers city centre is in map fold 5A

Variant
The main walk can easily be shortened by starting at a point on the edge of Béziers, by some fabulous canal locks – the Ecluses de Fonseranes (3) – and turning round at Colombiers (4).

the entrance to a public park in front, turn right and follow the Boulevard de Verdun down to a road junction. Turn right and go under a wide railway bridge.

Go past a roundabout and keep heading in the same direction. After a short distance, turn right and you will be walking with the **Canal du Midi** on your left. Pass alongside the Port Neuf. At its far end is a canal lock, which you pass to the right. After the short climb to the other side of the lock, you are on the canal towpath.

Follow the canal as it bears left and crosses the River Orb by means of a spectacular canal bridge (2). Continue alongside the canal for another kilometre or so. ▶ Approach the **Ecluses de Fonseranes** (3). At the foot of this striking series of canal locks, cross a footbridge, and turn left up a road which runs close to and parallel to the locks, with the locks on your left.

There are fine views to the right towards Béziers cathedral, standing high above the river.

The towpath continues into open country beyond the head of the locks. Follow this wide path, on the northern bank of the canal, all the way to the village of **Colombiers** (about 6km from the locks). Tall plane trees overhang the canal for most of its length.

You finally approach Colombiers (4). On the other side of the canal is a minor road leading towards the

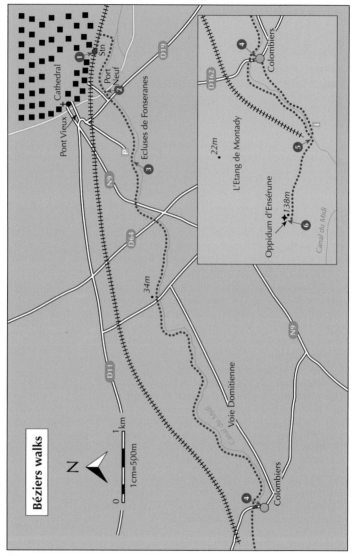

village, linking Colombiers and Béziers in a more or less dead straight line (shown on the 1:25,000 map as following the line of a Roman road, the Voie Domitienne). Also on the other side of the canal is a small port for pleasure boats. A little further on you come to an old stone road bridge over the canal. This is carrying the D162 road, which approaches Colombiers from the north. To enter the village, turn left, cross the bridge and you are in Colombiers.

From where the canal meets the D162 road, continue westwards along the north bank towpath of the canal. After about 1.5km, take a slip road on the right where the canal enters a cutting. You soon reach a road junction (5) just over a point where the canal, below, enters a short tunnel. Turn right up the winding road that leads to the **Oppidum d'Ensérune**. Near the end of this road a flight of steps takes you up a steep bank to the plateau where the archaeological site is located. The entrance to the main part (6) is a short distance away, on your left. ▶

There is a wonderful panorama from the Ensérune hillfort, the most remarkable feature being the **Etang de Montady**, to the north.

After touring the site, descend by the access road that you came up. At the foot of that road, you can either follow the towpath along the north bank of the canal, retracing your footsteps, or you can cross over and follow the canal on its south bank into Colombiers (4). Just after you cross the canal, there is a tourist information office on the right.

Return to Béziers from Colombiers by your outward route, along the north bank of the Canal du Midi.

Variant
Start at the Ecluses de Fonseranes (3). Follow the route of the walk described above, alongside the Canal du Midi, as far as Colombiers (4). Cross the bridge where the D162 road enters Colombiers and stroll around the village. Then return to the Ecluses de Fonseranes along the towpath.

POINTS OF INTEREST

Béziers: The heart of this large town is located on the site of a pre-Roman settlement. Its most prominent feature today is the cathedral, near which there is a fine viewpoint. The old town nearby is pleasant to wander around. In central Béziers there are also museums and, near the railway station, a charming landscaped park.

The Canal du Midi: Now classed as a World Heritage Site, this famous waterway was built in the 17th century by Pierre-Paul Riquet. He sank all his money into the project and died bankrupt just before the canal was completed. Riquet was born in Béziers; an imposing statue now stands in the central boulevard. Running from Toulouse to Sète, via Carcassonne and Béziers, the 240km canal established a link for commercial craft between the Atlantic and the Mediterranean, and is fed by water from springs rising in hills to the north. It is now used solely by leisure boats – but on a large scale. The towpath is also very popular with walkers and cyclists.

Looking towards the Etang de Montady from the pre-Roman Ensérune hillfort

The Ecluses (locks) de Fonseranes: Located on the western outskirts of Béziers, this is one of the most striking engineering works along the whole length of the Canal du Midi. It consists of a series of locks which enable boats to rise (or fall) by more than 20m in a distance of about 300m.

Colombiers: An attractive Mediterranean village lying alongside the Canal du Midi. It has a small port, with shops and bars alongside. Near the port is a tourist information office in a grand stone building.

The Oppidum (hillfort) d'Ensérune: Lying close to a principal Roman road (the Via Domitia, or Voie

Domitienne), these extensive remains have been described as one of the most outstanding archaeological sites in the south of France. This fortified site was first occupied in the 6th century BC. It continued in use for over a century after the Romans arrived and was abandoned in the 1st century AD. It has yielded an enormous number of artefacts and remains, many of which are displayed in a museum on the site. The delightful grounds have been planted with pine and cypress trees and several Mediterranean plants.

L'Etang de Montady: A large, roughly circular expanse of flat land divided into fields whose boundaries follow drainage ditches radiating out from the centre like the spokes of a bicycle wheel. *Etang* means 'pool' or 'lake', and a large body of water did lie to the north of Ensérune until the 13th century; its stagnant water was the cause of epidemics and it was drained in 1247. Its multi-coloured field pattern makes a very picturesque sight.

Visiting times
At least half a day is needed to do justice to Béziers cathedral and town centre. Allow at least 1hr to look around the Ensérune archaeological site and museum.

Further information
- Béziers tourist office: Palais des Congrès, 29 avenue St Saëns, 34500 Béziers; tel: (00 33) (0)4 67 76 84 00; tourisme@ville-beziers.fr; **www.ville-beziers.fr**.
- Colombiers tourist office: Maison du Tourisme, Hôtel de Ville, 34440 Colombiers; tel: (00 33) (0)4 67 37 00 90; maisontourisme.colombiers@wanadoo.fr; **www.colombiers.com**.
- Tourist office on the Canal du Midi below Ensérune hillfort: Maison du Malpas, Route de l'Oppidum, 34440 Colombiers; tel: (00 33) (0)4 67 32 88 77; maisondumalpas@wanadoo.fr; **www.lemalpas.com**.
- Ensérune hillfort (site and museum): Centre des monuments nationaux, Site et musée d'Ensérune, 34400 Nissan-lez-Ensérune: tel: (00 33) (0)4 67 37 01 23; **www.monum.fr**.
- Canal du Midi: **www.lecanaldumidi.com**.

2 MINERVE

This section describes a long walk and a short walk. Both are circular, and start in the village of Minerve.

The long walk crosses a very dry limestone landscape, the *causse*, and passes close to two dolmens. The short walk passes the reconstructed 'Malvoisine' (see below). Both cross riverbeds in the gorges near Minerve. Those are usually dry in the summer, but in the winter, and at other times after heavy rain, the rivers flow. The long walk is best not attempted in these circumstances; most of the short walk can be followed, but from a different starting point.

Of all the landscapes encountered in this book, that around Minerve is the driest and most Mediterranean in character.

CATHAR HISTORY: JULY 1210

After the sack of Béziers, the French army moved west to besiege the key fortress of Carcassonne. The Viscount of Carcassonne allowed the crusaders to take complete control of the town without a fight.

An enormous task still lay ahead for the French invaders. They had to quash resistance in the surrounding countryside and suppress the Cathar church in its entirety.

Some of the leading French barons were eager to return to their domains in the north. Thus Amaury appointed as long-term military chief of the crusade – and as the new Viscount of Carcassonne – a minor French noble, Simon de Montfort (father of another Simon de Montfort, earl of Leicester, who, later in the 13th century, played a leading role in establishing the first English parliament.)

De Montfort proved to be a brilliant, ambitious and ruthless military leader of the crusade against the Cathars. In the years following the fall of Carcassonne, he almost constantly travelled around Languedoc, capturing castles, suppressing revolt and burning heretics.

Some castles surrendered without a fight (such as Villerouge-Termenès – see Section 14). Others, such was Minerve, situated on a clifftop at the junction of two river gorges some 35km northeast of Carcassonne, put up strong resistance.

Montfort and his army besieged Minerve in the summer of 1210. They bombarded it mercilessly with huge stones fired by giant catapults. A reconstruction of the most formidable of those catapults – the 'Malvoisine' ('bad neighbour') – can be seen opposite the town today. With this deadly weapon, Montfort eventually destroyed a staircase giving access to the town's well, near the junction of the two river gorges.

Deprived of water and food, the defenders of Minerve were forced to capitulate. On 22 July, after a siege lasting more than five weeks, the crusaders' army entered the town. About 150 Cathars who refused to renounce their faith were thrown onto the flames of a huge fire just outside the town.

Later events

Minerve castle was subsequently occupied by the French forces. Once Languedoc had been fully subdued by the French crown, the castle's military significance declined. Time, weather and neglect then took their toll, and the fortress was finally demolished in the 17th century.

Minerve: the slender tower on the left is all that remains of the Cathar castle here

PRACTICAL INFORMATION
Access to starting points

Both walks start on the graceful, high, arched bridge which spans the Cesse gorge and which leads into Minerve village from the south. By motor vehicle, Minerve is best approached either from Carcassonne (via the D610 going towards Béziers, then north through Olonzac) or from Narbonne (via the D607 through St-Marcel-sur-Aude). Visitors' vehicles are not allowed into Minerve village. Use the car park on the D10 near the bridge into Minerve. Alternatively, there is a higher car park to the north of the village, by the D147.

Public transport is very scarce in this area.

To undertake the short walk when water is flowing

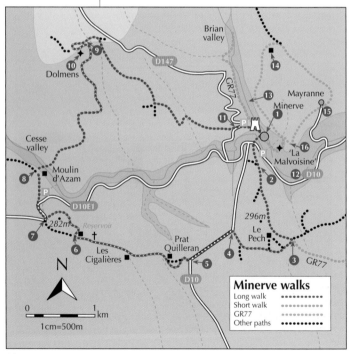

through the gorge below Minerve, travel eastwards along the D10, then turn left up a minor road to Mayranne, near (15). The walk can be started and finished there, avoiding the gorge between the 'Malvoisine' and Minerve.

Navigation

The first part of the long walk follows the GR77, indicated by red and white waymarks, followed by a stretch of road walking (not waymarked). After that the route is indicated by small, green metal posts (with occasional yellow painted waymarks), indicating a wider, local 'green network' of trails which is open to walkers, cyclists and horse-riders.

Almost the whole of the short walk is indicated by yellow waymarks. At one or two track junctions look very carefully for a waymark showing you which way to go.

ROUTE DESCRIPTION – LONG WALK

Distance:	18km (11.2 miles)
Time:	5hr
Altitude:	180m to 400m
Map:	IGN 1:25,000 2444ET (Somail Minervois); Minerve is in map fold 2

From the bridge leading to **Minerve** (1), turn away from the village and, beyond the bridge, follow a path up an embankment which lies straight ahead. At the top there is a sign for the GR77 path. Follow that sign across the road and onto a track going up the hillside opposite.

After passing a couple of buildings, the track becomes a stony path and climbs into open countryside. As the path traverses the hillside, there are splendid views back towards Minerve. The path meets a tarmacked lane (2). Continue uphill along that lane (ignore an unsurfaced track going off left). There is a fine limestone wall on your right. When the surfaced lane swings to the right, continue straight ahead onto an unsurfaced track.

Reach the top of the hill and pass alongside vineyards. Ignore a track going towards a stone building (Le Pech) on the right. Your track soon starts to descend the other side of the hill, and views far to the south suddenly appear. On a clear day, these extend right across the Corbières hills to Canigou and other Pyrenees mountains in the far distance.

Meet a tarmacked lane (3). Turn right, leaving the GR77, which continues straight ahead. Keep to this lane as it heads roughly westwards, dipping and weaving. Ignore other lanes and tracks going off to right and left – keep to the principal lane. The lane is not waymarked, but its route is obvious.

Shortly after turning sharp right, the lane descends to meet the D10 (4). Ahead you can see the Cesse valley – a limestone gorge – snaking through the landscape from west to east. Above that is a sloping plateau (**causse**), entirely covered in Mediterranean scrub vegetation. In the far distance is higher ground in the direction of the Montagne Noire.

The sun sets on the scant remains of the Cathar castle in Minerve

Now turn left and walk alongside the D10 for about 10min. There may not be a lot of motor traffic, but what there is could be moving quite fast, so take care. There are walkable verges alongside most stretches of this road. Occasional small green posts indicate that you are now on a local waymarked route for walkers and cyclists.

Shortly after the road – going downhill – turns to the left, turn sharp right onto a narrow tarmacked lane (5). Follow this lane for some distance. There should be very little motor traffic on it, but look out for passing vehicles. Short green posts continue to waymark your route.

The lane bends to the left and comes to a fork, with a stately stone building up on the right. Take the left fork, ignoring immediately afterwards a track going off on the left. The lane swings to the right, then passes to the left of the stately stone building (Prat Quilleran). ▶

The occupants of Prat Quilleran claim that the lane passing the front of their house is private property.

The lane passes through a cluster of impressive pine trees, then approaches buildings, Les Cigalières. Look out for old wine-pressing machines and barrels by the road, and notices in nearby vineyards telling you which types of grapes are grown. Pass to the right of those buildings.

The lane descends a little and you pass, on your right, an elaborately worked metal cross on an upturned boulder. Shortly after that, as you approach some houses, yellow waymarks tell you to turn right, off the lane onto an unsurfaced track going uphill (6). Following this track, pass to the left of a covered reservoir at the top of the hill, then swing to the left. The track becomes a path; follow this as it weaves downhill a little. Other tracks and paths go off from your path here and there, so be careful to follow the yellow waymarks (the best-trodden route). ▶

There are excellent views to the right, across the cliffs of the Cesse gorge, to the gently sloping *causse* plateau. A track climbing out of the gorge and up that hill marks your route a little later on.

Your path curves around the right-hand edge of a stretch of open ground, then descends to meet the D10E1 on a sharp bend (7). Turn right and follow that road as it descends, quite steeply, along the bottom of a small valley.

Where the road bends to the right, carry straight on along a track which immediately passes to the left of a car park and picnic spot. You are now walking straight towards the gorge. When you reach the top of a cliff on the edge of the gorge, the track you have been following swings to the left. Take what is initially a grass track going down on the right (8), ignoring a yellow painted cross nearby. It soon becomes a stony path, which zigzags down the side of the gorge.

Just before reaching the bottom of the gorge, pass to the right of a small stone building, an old mill, the Moulin d'Azam. ▶

Inside the Moulin d'Azam there is an old millstone lying in the sand on the floor; just outside, on the right, is another, half-buried millstone.

Cross the floor of the valley.

You will see that the lower part of some steps built into the other side of the gorge have been washed away, but you can take a stony path to the right of the steps. This path soon swings back and comes out at the top of the steps. Follow the stony path ahead, which winds steeply up the side of the gorge. The path is not dangerous, but there is a steep drop to the right, so take care.

The path soon emerges at the top of the gorge. It then becomes a wide track, climbing steadily for some distance up the hillside ahead. There is spiky, impenetrable vegetation on all sides. Ignore less well-marked tracks which occasionally go off from this one. Small green posts along the track once again show which route to follow.

You eventually reach a clearing where another track goes off to the left (9). Turn left onto that track, noting that you will shortly return to this point. Not far along that track, you will see on the left a path cutting across the scrub, which leads after a short distance to a dolmen (10). ◀

The entrance chamber faces the sun, looking towards the distant hills and mountains. A little further on, after a small dip, lies another dolmen, reached by a short path left.

From the **dolmens**, return to the track junction at the clearing (9), and turn left. The track you have now regained soon swings to the right. Shortly after that, at a track crossing, be careful to turn right, and head south, downhill. Once again the small green posts indicate the route to take. Another deep gorge quickly opens up on the right (ignore another track which forks to the right and starts to go down into that gorge).

Follow the track all the way downhill back towards Minerve. On a clear day the extensive view to the south is mesmerisingly beautiful. The track forks and twists at various points, but its route is always clearly indicated by the small green posts and it is generally the best-used and most obvious route. Eventually you approach some vineyards and isolated buildings. Here the track swings left, crosses a valley, then swings right. It is joined by other tracks coming from nearby buildings on both sides and becomes a tarmacked lane. After rounding a left bend, Minerve suddenly comes into view – and a superb sight it is, too.

The lane reaches the D147 (11), where you turn left. Where the road very soon bends left uphill, go straight on to cross a large car park opposite. Shortly after leaving the car park, the road you are on approaches a sharp left bend. But before going down there, you may like to take a path going alongside some pine trees on the right. After a few metres you reach the top of a very steep slope from where there is possibly the finest view of all of Minerve. The solitary stone tower (the 'Candela') of the fortification which sheltered the Cathars is on the left, the church stands out prominently in the centre, and below is the magnificent arched bridge across the Cesse gorge.

Return to the road and follow it as it bends to the left. It very soon swings to the right (from where, incidentally, the GR77 on the left heads north, along the side of the Brian gorge). The road then brings you back into Minerve village (1).

ROUTE DESCRIPTION – SHORT WALK

Distance:	6km (3.7 miles)
Time:	2hr
Altitude:	150m to 340m
Map:	as for long walk

Cross the bridge and enter the village of **Minerve** (1). As you do, note the Chemin de ronde running along the foot of the cliffs below the bridge. Make your way down to that path by turning right when you enter the village, then go right again a little further on. Go down some steps, which take you to the Chemin de ronde.

There, turn left. ▶

You soon come to the point where the Brian riverbed meets that of the Cesse. You will see, just below the Chemin de ronde, the well – Puits de St-Rustique – the destruction of which by Simon de Montfort's besieging army led to the downfall of Minerve.

Head straight across the dry riverbed and cross a footbridge, which reaches the foot of the cliff on the

Across the valley floor, on the right, is the entrance to the first and longer of two amazing *ponts naturels* – 'natural bridges' – below Minerve.

One of the ponts naturels (natural bridges, or tunnels) close to Minerve through which the Cesse river runs in winter

other side of the valley. Climb the path, which takes you to the top of cliff. When you emerge you will see, just on your left, a reconstruction of the catapult – the 'Malvoisine' – used in the siege of 1210 to bombard the well below (12).

You have an excellent view of Minerve opposite, perched on a narrow natural promontory high above the two converging riverbeds. With the valley on your left, and a vineyard on your right, walk along the track past the Malvoisine. After a short distance, branch left where the track forks. Continue on this track for some distance as it runs close to the valley's eastern clifftop, with Minerve sitting impressively on the cliff opposite.

Where the track starts to veer away from the valley, take a careful step or two to the left to peer over the edge of the cliff (13). The depth of the valley, with its nearly sheer limestone cliffs, is striking.

The track climbs and passes, on your right, an isolated but pretty smallholding (14). The track then curves to the right and joins a minor road. Turn right onto that road and follow it as it descends steadily towards the hamlet of Mayranne. You should have straight ahead a fine view over the hilly Minervois land-scape – a patchwork of carefully tended vineyards and olive groves surrounded by bone-dry ***causse***.

Follow the road as it bends to the right and passes through Mayranne. Be careful to take a track which forks off on the right (15), while the minor road heads down towards the valley on the left.

The track climbs a little, then starts to descend. As it does so – and probably with the roofs of Minerve becoming just visible again on the right – watch carefully for a path which descends, sharp right (16), off the track which you are on. Turn down there. You soon rejoin the track you took on your outward journey, just above the Malvoisine.

From there, go left and follow the track past the Malvoisine. Then turn right down the path which descends the cliff. Cross the riverbed and retrace your steps back into Minerve (1).

POINTS OF INTEREST

Minerve village: Despite being devoted to tourism, the village has retained its unspoilt, historic character. It has been designated as one of 'the most beautiful villages of France'. All that remains of the medieval fortifications is the tall, slender 'Candela' at its northern end, and sections of the town's walls lower down.

The village has two museums. One is devoted to local geology and archaeology (traces of prehistoric man have been found in a nearby cave); the other (the Musée Hurepel, open only in the summer) deals with the Cathar legend. The local tourist office has details of guided tours of the village and its church.

The moving sculpture next to the village church, which depicts the Cathar faith, was created by local sculptor Jean-Paul Séverac in 1982. It is a large, upright slab of rock, pierced right through by the outline of a dove. The artist described it as 'a sculpture of light; a monument to peace'.

The ponts naturels: 40m-high gorges, whose walls are vertical lime-stone cliffs, have been carved into the plateaux surrounding Minerve. At two places close to the village in the Cesse gorge, underground passages in the limestone have been enlarged and linked up to allow the river to cut off former meanders in the valley. These now form natural tunnels or bridges and can be walked through in dry conditions. The western tunnel is about 100m long and 15m high; the bigger, eastern one is 250m long and up to 40m high.

The dolmens: At the highest point on the long walk, in grand isolation on a limestone plateau and facing the Pyrenees mountains far to the south, are two impressive dolmens. These megalithic tombs are said to be around 4000 years old.

The *causse*: An especially arid type of limestone landscape, which covers extensive areas in various parts of southeast France. Apart from occasional low trees and bushes such as evergreen oak and juniper, the often-sparse vegetation generally stays close to the surface. Fragrant thyme and rosemary can be abundant, but one of the most typical and widespread plants is the ciste, or rock rose, which has pink-red flowers.

Visiting time
Minerve village is not very large, and hardly any of its castle survives, but it is a charming and fascinating place, with two small museums. Allow half a day if you can.

Further information
- Minerve tourist office (Syndicat d'initiative): 9, rue des Martyrs, 34210 Minerve; tel: (00 33) (0)4 68 91 8143; minerve.accueil@wanadoo.fr; **www.ot-herault.com/minerve**.
- These two walks are based on those in a locally available book *L'échappée belle en Minervois*, published in 1998 by the Syndicat Intercommunal Cesse et Brian, 34210 Siran; tel: (00 33) (0)4 68 91 55 59. In French, it is particularly informative about local flowers, trees and other plants.

3 LASTOURS

A long walk and a short walk are suggested in this section. The long walk follows a figure-of-eight route (either one of its two loops could also be used a shorter walk); the short walk is a circular route.

The long walk starts from les Ilhes, a village about 2km north of Lastours. It does not pass very close to Lastours, but there are good views of the castles in the distance. The route follows an ancient path across steep hillsides covered in Mediterranean vegetation; then it crosses higher, open ground which is grazed by livestock and from which, in clear weather, there are superlative panoramas as far as the Pyrenees. There are two long climbs.

The short walk starts and finishes in Lastours village, immediately below the castles. It passes close to a *belvédère* (viewpoint) from where there is a justly renowned panorama of the castles.

CATHAR HISTORY: MARCH 1211

The remains of four medieval castles run along the spine of a rocky ridge towering above the present-day village of Lastours. They present one of the most striking sights in Cathar castle country. Three of the castles were in existence in the early 13th century when they belonged to a powerful, war-like but cultured clan of barons led by Pierre-Roger de Cabaret. The barons strongly supported the Cathars and gave them shelter. They also put up fierce resistance to de Montfort's forces and harassed them mercilessly.

De Montfort besieged the Lastours fortresses in late 1209, but failed to take them. However, in subsequent months he had great success in taking control of other castles in the region. De Cabaret decided to seek a negotiated settlement with de Montfort, with the result that the Cathars departed from Lastours and the French army took control of the castles peacefully in early 1211.

Later events
During a Cathar resurgence in the years following de Montfort's death in 1218, de Cabaret reoccupied Lastours. The castles once again became a bastion of the Cathar faith, but were seized by the French in 1229 and their Cathar occupants were forced to flee. The fortified village which then existed

The Lastours castles, as seen from the belvédère (viewpoint) on the short walk

close to the castles at the northern end of the ridge was destroyed (its remains are being excavated today). The castles were reconstructed and survived for another five centuries, finally falling into ruin after the French Revolution.

PRACTICAL INFORMATION

Access to starting points

Les Ilhes village is about 15km north of Carcassonne. By road from Carcassonne, head north on the D149 to Conques-sur-Orbiel. From there, follow the D101 up the Orbiel valley. About 2km after passing through Lastours village, you reach les Ilhes. There is a car park on the left; the walk starts by a map board on the other side of the road.

The short walk starts at the visitor centre (a former textile mill) in Lastours village. Park in the large car park on the right as you enter the village. The visitor centre is a little further along the main road (the D101) through Lastours.

Public transport is scarce in this area.

Navigation

Yellow painted rectangles are the waymarks to look out for on both walks. There are some others (around les

Ilhes in particular) and they are best ignored. In a few places (as indicated in the route descriptions), there are no waymarks where they would be especially useful, so take care at such points.

On the long walk, the path follows the floor of a deep valley between Limousis and Fournes-Cabardès. This is normally dry, but it is evident from the debris scattered about the valley floor that it can soon fill up with water during or after heavy rainfall. Avoid that section of the walk in such weather.

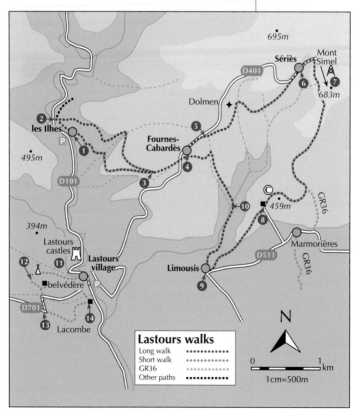

ROUTE DESCRIPTION – LONG WALK

Distance:	16km (9.9 miles)
Time:	6hr (les Ilhes to Fournes-Cabardès circuit 2.5hr; Fournes-Cabardès to Limousis circuit 3.5hr)
Altitude:	240m to 680m
Map:	IGN 1:25,000 2345 est (Carcassonne)

From the D101 in les Ilhes, by a small fountain and a map board (1), cross the Orbiel river by the green metal bridge. Shortly after entering the village on the other side, turn left and walk to the far end of the village.

At the end of the village, follow the cobbled track as it starts to climb the slope on the right. Ignore a turning on the right. Pass through a cleft in a spur of rock, then reach a junction with a jeep track (2). Turn sharp right. You are on an old mule track between the Orbiel valley villages and settlements on higher ground.

This track climbs steadily. Excellent views south to the towers of **Lastours castles** soon appear. Further on, the track narrows, but it is always easy to follow. ◀

On a clear day you may also be able to make out the distinctive profile of the Pech de Bugarach in the far distance, almost directly behind the Lastours towers.

After turning left around a distinctive hill spur, the path descends gently towards a valley bottom on the right. It crosses that, swerves to the right, then starts a long, hard climb around the next hill spur. Eventually the slope levels out. You may now start to see the eastern Pyrenees in the far distance, on the right. This very fine view is one which, in clear weather, you will enjoy for a substantial part of this walk.

The track swings right and descends. Note a path going off sharp right (3). Later on it will be your route back to les Ilhes. But for now, keep to the main path as it bends left and soon descends into another valley, on the right. There you join a concrete track, with vegetable gardens on the right. Follow the concrete track up the valley towards the village of Fournes-Cabardès, now clearly visible straight ahead.

On entering the village (4), follow the rue de la Voute round to the right. Then swing to the left, uphill into the rue de la Fontaine. Most of the village is on your left. At a crossroads, with a *lavoir* (washing-place) on the other side of the road on the left, note a lane coming in from the right alongside open fields. From this point you follow a wide loop which will in due course bring you back here, via the lane on the right.

For the moment carry on straight ahead, up the minor road which winds out of the village. Just after leaving the village and reaching open ground, ignore a smaller motor road going off on the left and keep to the road you are on for a few minutes more. Then note a turning off to the right along a waymarked grass lane (5).

The remains of a large dolmen are on a hillock just to the right of the D401 about 10min beyond point 5. If you walk along that road to visit the monument, it is best to return along the same road to point 5 to resume the walk, rather than try to cut directly across rough country to pick up the path further along. Alternatively, you can continue walking along the road and pick up the route described below in Sériès.

From point 5 the track ahead is very pleasant, with wonderful views. Shortly after climbing through woodland, the lane rejoins the road, on the left. Keep heading in the same direction and follow the road down through the hamlet of Sériès (6). At the bottom of the hill, the road crosses a small valley, bends to the right and starts to go uphill. Where the road swerves left, with a large building on the left, leave the road and take a track going off on the right.

The track climbs steadily and reaches a crossing on open ground on the shoulder of Mont Simel. This is the highest point on the walk, but you may want to stroll up and back to the hilltop on the left (7), where there is a large pylon. From there you have an even wider view. All around is the high ground of the **Cabardès** region; to the east you look straight down towards the coastal plains near Narbonne; to the south is the lower ground of the Aude valley, in the vicinity of **Carcassonne**.

Return to the track crossing and carry straight on in the direction you were going, over to the other side of the ridge.

The track, now wide and stony, goes downhill. The village you are heading for, Limousis, comes into view straight ahead. Eventually the track bends to the left and goes downhill more steeply, with a valley falling away on your left. Towards the bottom of the slope, take a right fork and follow the track as it now bends round to the right. After crossing a shallow valley, ignore tracks going off on the left and fork right, uphill once again. There is a cairn on a small hill at 459m ahead. Pass to the right of that hill, but again you may want to go out and back to that hilltop for the view, which is now over the compact little village of Marmorières, directly below (on the GR36 long-distance footpath).

The track you are on becomes a narrow path, which weaves downhill on the right through dense undergrowth. Keep to that path, and in particular keep well away from a fenced-off quarry higher up on the left. Suddenly the path emerges at the end of a small surfaced road with, immediately on your right, the entrance to a cave, the **Grotte de Limousis**. You have to pay to enter the cave; the ticket office is a little way down the road, on the left. Walk past the ticket office, then turn right at the road T-junction (8) a little way beyond.

This road eventually brings you down to the village of Limousis (9). Turn right at a road junction shortly after entering the village (a church is on the left). A little further on, turn right into the village's small square and take the street going straight ahead out of the village, just to the left of a belfry, with limestone crags in the distance beyond. The street becomes a stone track, which bends right and goes down into the deep valley below.

Your route now follows the valley bottom, up the valley. Watch carefully for the point where the valley bends to the right and your path (waymarked) goes up on the left (10), on a line just above and to the right of the bottom of a tributary valley. You now have a long climb up this path, which is soon joined by another, on

Walkers near Limousis, which is passed on the long walk

the right, and becomes a track. With (quite possibly) the sun on your back, this is the hardest section of the walk, so take your time.

After a long haul, the track bends left and crosses the head of the tributary valley that you have been walking parallel to. The slope levels out and Fournes-Cabardès comes into view just beyond the fields ahead. Follow the track into the village (4).

Come to the crossroads with the washing-place on the right. Turn left here and retrace your earlier route down through the village and onto the concrete track (signposted as le Carral) going out of the village with cultivated gardens on the left. Fork right onto the unsurfaced track that brought you from les Ilhes. Follow that track to the point where the footpath for the return route to les Ilhes forks off to the left (3). Take that path. There is little waymarking along it, but this is hardly necessary because the route is easy to follow. It winds down the long steep slope, which falls into the Orbiel valley far beneath you on the left.

As the path approaches les Ilhes, you catch glimpses of the village far below. The path enters the village by a delightful cobbled lane. Turn right at the end of that lane and go past a fine half-timbered building. Turn left to cross the bridge over the river and thus return to the starting point of the walk (1).

ROUTE DESCRIPTION – SHORT WALK

Distance:	4km (2.5 miles)
Time:	2hr
Altitude:	230m to 320m
Map:	as for long walk

This walk is depicted on a large map in the car park at the southern end of the village.

From the visitor centre in **Lastours village** (11), walk back down the road a short way to where the road bends to the left on crossing a small stream. On the stream bank by the road, as you face upstream, you will see a yellow waymark. Walk into the valley, alongside the left-hand side of the stream, following the waymarks and guide rails.

After the first, slightly slippery section of the walk, the path bears left up the valley side and climbs steeply through the woods. It emerges at the top, opposite a fenced campsite. Turn right here, along a track that soon bears left around the perimeter of the campsite. At a junction with a narrow metalled road (12), turn left.

After passing a football pitch on your left, turn left through an olive grove. At the bottom, turn left again and visit the *belvédère* on the top of the hill opposite the castles. ◀

En route for the *belvédère* you pass through a cabin where you will need to pay or show your castle entrance ticket.

Return to the road at the foot of the olive grove, and follow it downhill to a road T-junction. Go up the road straight ahead. At the top of the rise, turn left (13) along a lane which winds around the edge of the hill, heading for the hamlet of Lacombe.

On reaching Lacombe (14), go to the right of some of the buildings, then turn left, downhill, along a path between buildings (one being in a ruined state). The path may be a little overgrown just here, but it soon broadens out. The path bears to the left, crosses a small valley, and climbs up to the rue du Belvédère, close to a church.

Here, turn sharp right and go down that road as it swings to the left through Lastours and descends to the valley bottom. Turn left on reaching the D101 road there. The visitor centre at the start of the walk (11) is only a short distance away.

The northernmost of the four Lastours castles, Cabaret

Lastours castles: There are the remains of four castles here: (from south to north) Quertinheux, Surdespine, Tour Régine and Cabaret. Tour Régine, the smallest, was built after the French crusaders' conquest of Languedoc.

At the time of writing, adults have to pay 4 Euros to enter the site of the Lastours castles (from the visitor centre). You also have to pay to gain access to the *belvédère* on the short walk, but a ticket to the castles will give you free access. There are reductions for groups, and guided visits for groups can also be arranged. The visitor centre is said to be open every day from April to October inclusive, and at weekends during the rest of the year (except January, when it is closed). *Son et lumière* displays from the *belvédère* are arranged in July and August.

The Cabardès: A region of deep, narrow valleys and surrounding hills which extend from the heights of the Montagne Noire, at an altitude of about 1200m in the north, to the lowlands near Carcassonne in the south. The north–south-orientated Orbiel valley, in which Lastours and les Ilhes are located, is the longest valley in the Cabardès. The region has a Mediterranean aspect, with vineyards and former olive groves on its southern slopes. Today it is much more sparsely populated than in previous centuries; everywhere in the hills are signs of earlier occupation and human activity, from dolmens and other prehistoric remains, to former churches, chapels, castles, farmsteads and mines.

Carcassonne: Although this huge fortress was taken by the French in 1209, support for the Cathar church lingered here to the very end. In 1329, four Cathar believers were caught in Carcassonne and burnt at the stake. It was the last such execution of Cathars in Languedoc.

Today, the fortress in Carcassonne is referred to as la Cité, to distinguish it from the town on the other side of the Aude river (the latter is known as the Ville Basse – lower town).

La Cité is a World Heritage Site and is the largest and best-preserved medieval fortress in Europe. Today's fortified town is mainly the result of three periods of building: that undertaken in the 11th and 12th centuries; the addition of a second wall and other works by the French when they took over Carcassonne following the crusade against the Cathars; and extensive restoration work supervised by Viollet-le-Duc in the 19th century. This colossal monument is a wonderful sight, with its dream-like spires, double line of high defensive walls, imposing gateways, castle, narrow medieval streets, tightly packed houses, and 13th-century church with superb stained-glass windows.

The Ville Basse was also once a fortified town with enclosing walls. Wide boulevards following the line of those former ramparts now enclose it. The streets have a rectangular pattern. It is a partially pedestrianised commercial centre with squares, churches and an art gallery, all worth visiting. The Canal du Midi passes along the northern edge of the Ville Basse. The port on the canal, close to the railway station, is a colourful sight.

Grotte de Limousis: A series of limestone caves with remarkable rock formations. It extends under the hillside for over 500m.

Lastours village: Tightly wedged in the bottom of the narrow Orbiel valley, this settlement lies directly below the castles. Like other villages in this area, its past economic activity was industrial as well as agricultural. Mines and quarries have been worked in the surrounding hills for centuries: for iron, copper, silver and even gold. The large former factory in Lastours, with its tall chimney, was formerly used for textile manufacture. It is now a visitor centre, which serves as the entrance to the castles and which offers a modern exhibition about Lastours' distant and recent past.

Visiting times
Lastours castles and visitor centre: allow at least 2hr. Grotte de Limousis: allow 1hr.

Further information
- Lastours visitor centre: Châteaux de Lastours, Accueil Usine Rabier, 11600 Lastours; tel: (00 33) (0)04 68 77 56 02; chateaux.lastours@online.fr; **chateauxlastours.lwd.fr**.
- The long walk is a combination of a circular walk from les Ilhes to Fournes-Cabardès published in *Les Sentiers d'Emile en Pays cathare* and one from Fournes-Cabardès to Limousis published in the FFRP's *Topo-guide, L'Aude, Pays Cathare à pied*. See Appendix 1.
- A locally available booklet in French, entitled simply *Le Cabardès*, by Marie-Elise Gardel (Aude Aménagement, 11855 Carcassonne Cedex 9, 1998), is a very good source of information about the geology, landscape and history of Lastours and its surrounding area. The author has led the archaeological excavations at Lastours for some years.

4 FOIX

This section offers a long, linear walk and a short, out-and-back-walk.

The long walk starts in the small town of Montgaillard, about 4km south-southeast of Foix, and ends in Foix town centre. The route follows waymarked paths across the broad Ariège valley alongside hay meadows, before climbing steeply onto a rocky, open ridge, where it meets the Sentier Cathare long-distance path. Finally it follows the Sentier Cathare as it descends steeply through woodland to Foix.

The short walk follows the Sentier Cathare. It climbs steadily from Foix up to an open ridge, then returns by the same route.

From the high ground on both walks there are superb panoramas south and west towards the Pyrenees and north towards the Toulouse lowlands.

CATHAR HISTORY: 1210–18

We now head southwest to the city of Foix. In doing so, we cross a long, low-lying corridor of land which extends from Toulouse to Carcassonne, scene of many critical events during the crusade against the Cathars.

One such place is Bram, close to the Canal du Midi and almost on the direct line between Lastours and Foix. In April 1210, during his campaign of suppressing resistance to the crusade, Simon de Montfort was angered by the defiance of the people of Bram. When he finally took the town, he took 100 men from his prisoners and had their eyes pulled out and noses cut off. Those poor wretches then marched in a pitiful procession to Lastours, led by a man who had been left with just one eye.

An event of very great significance –a major turning point in the histories of France and Spain – took place a short distance to the south of Toulouse in September 1213. This was the Battle of Muret, the biggest single military confrontation in the century-long campaign against the Cathars in Languedoc.

Not for the first time, de Montfort's forces were greatly outnumbered by their opponents. The latter consisted of a coalition of troops from both sides of the Pyrenees led by King Pere (Peter) of Aragon. Recently victorious in a battle against the Moors, Pere was confident of victory against de Montfort. But he exposed himself to unnecessary risk and was killed in the fighting; news of his death spread panic in the coalition's camp. Lacking decisive leadership, they broke up and retreated towards Toulouse in disarray. De Montfort's forces pursued and massacred them without respite. The crusaders' victory was complete.

Those few hours of pitched battle south of Toulouse had geopolitical consequences. Not only was the Cathars' downfall almost irredeemably sealed, the way was also open for the kingdom of France to extend its territory once and for all southwards towards the Pyrenees. This it did in subsequent decades.

Meanwhile Raymond-Roger, Count of Foix, was one of de Montfort's most formidable opponents. His sympathies were clearly with the Cathars (his sister Esclarmonde was a *Bonne Femme*). Raymond-Roger's principal sanctuary was the castle of Foix.

In the months following the Battle of Muret, de Montfort extended his domain and became ever more powerful. Faced with this situation, and in an effort to gain favour with Pope Innocent III, Raymond-Roger handed over his castle to the pope's legate in 1215. As a military threat to de Montfort, Foix castle was thus neutralised.

De Montfort now seemed invincible. But the people of Languedoc were far from completely crushed; from 1216, and led now by the Count of Toulouse's son, they inflicted a number of setbacks on the occupying army. This culminated in de Montfort being killed during a skirmish just outside Toulouse in June 1218.

In the same year, the Count of Foix had little trouble in recovering his castle.

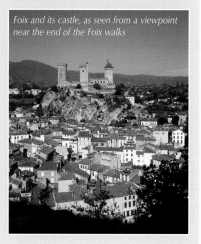

Foix and its castle, as seen from a viewpoint near the end of the Foix walks

Later events

Foix castle remained a centre of resistance to the French on and off during the 13th century, ending in 1272 after a successful siege led by the French king himself. The castle's key strategic position, on an almost impregnable site in the Ariège valley leading to Spain, caused it to retain a military function right up to the 18th century. It was constantly repaired and modified and not allowed to fall into ruin, like most other fortifications in Cathar castle country. It became a prison in the 18th century and was designated an historic monument in 1862. Restoration work has been carried out on the castle since that date.

PRACTICAL INFORMATION
Access to starting points

Foix is on a main railway line, connecting Toulouse to Barcelona. It is also served by long-distance bus services along the Ariège valley. The main road along the valley now bypasses Foix to the east, but the old main road, the N20, gives access to the town centre.

Montgaillard can be reached from Foix by bus, train or taxi. Local bus services radiate out of Foix town centre. In particular, line 5 of the Foix Navette Interurbaine service runs from just outside the tourist office to the Place du Scios in the centre of Montgaillard, where the long walk starts. The tourist office in Foix is on the main, north–south thoroughfare through the town centre, the Cours Gabriel Fauré. It is close to a covered market hall, the Halle aux Grains. The *navettes* (minibuses) run every day except on Sundays and public holidays, and there are about three buses in the morning. Timetables are available from the tourist office. There are also a few long-distance bus services (and an infrequent rail service) along the Ariège valley linking Foix and Montgaillard.

The taxi fare from Foix to Montgaillard is about 10 Euros. Taxis leave from the Halle aux Grains in the centre of Foix.

Navigation

From the start of the long walk in Montgaillard (1) to point (11), the route follows paths on local circuits, indicated with yellow painted waymarks. A short section from point (11) to the col de Porte Pa (12) is unwaymarked but easy to follow. From the col to Foix, the route follows the Sentier Cathare, indicated with red and yellow painted waymarks.

The short walk follows the Sentier Cathare.

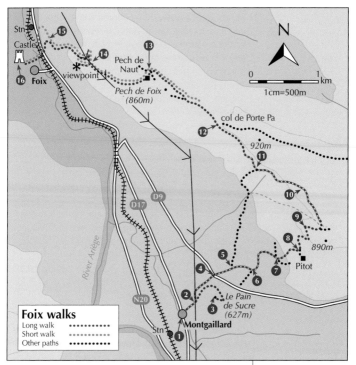

ROUTE DESCRIPTION – LONG WALK

Distance:	14km (8.7 miles)
Time:	5hr
Altitude:	370m to 850m
Map:	IGN 1:25,000 2147ET (Foix Tarascon-sur-Ariège); Foix is in map fold 2C

From the Place du Scios in Montgaillard (1), with a river on your right, walk across to the far right-hand corner of the square. Go through a short alley and soon reach a much larger square with a church and a school on the left. Cross to the far left-hand corner of the square. A wooden path waymark points away from Montgaillard towards the hills beyond. Head in that direction, passing a handsome old *château* on the right as you leave the town. The tarmacked lane which you are on bends to the left, and a waymarked green lane goes up on the half-right (2).

To walk to the top of the 'Sugar Loaf' (the *pain de sucre*), follow that way-marked green lane. It curves around the hillside, climbing through woodland all the while. On the other side of the hill, the waymarked route suddenly turns right and starts to zigzag steeply up the hillside. Emerge into the open, upper part of the hill. The path turns to the right and climbs towards the summit (3) – a very fine viewpoint. To the west and south are the high Ariège mountains. Montgaillard and the **Ariège valley** are at your feet, and **Foix** is spread out to the north. You can also trace, across the countryside to the east, the route of the next part of this walk towards the craggy ridge beyond.

There is at least one other path to the summit so, on descending, take care to pick up the waymarked path that you took on the way up. Follow it back down to the country road you left earlier on (2).

Continue along the country road away from Montgaillard. It curves around the base of the 'Sugar Loaf', then comes to a crossing with the D9 road (4).

Part of the next section, although waymarked and on a local walking route, has been known to be heavily overgrown. If you don't want to take the risk, turn right and walk along the D9 for a little way, then turn left onto a surfaced lane which is soon joined by the main route at point (6).

From the crossing with the D9 (4), take an access track opposite, indicated with a wooden path waymark, which begins by a picnic site. It passes a modern agricultural building on the left, then becomes a grassy lane.

You soon come to a track intersection (5). Turn right here (to follow the local circuit in the opposite direction to that described in an FFRP *Topo-guide* – some waymark arrows will be pointing in the direction you have just come!). ▶

You are now walking up a sunken lane. It soon turns to the left and emerges into open country. It is from here in particular that it may become overgrown. It eventually joins a surfaced lane at a sharp corner in that lane (6).

Go straight ahead onto that lane. Follow it as it winds up the slope ahead, passing meadows on both sides. Foix castle can be seen far over to the left; look back to see the whole of the 'Sugar Loaf' hill.

Where the lane turns sharp left, with a farm track signposted for Pitot straight ahead (7), take a waymarked path half-left. That path climbs up the right-hand side of a field in which trees have been planted. Head straight for the steep, craggy scarp beyond the enclosed fields and trees.

Eventually pass through a metal gate where you turn half-right across an enclosure with scattered oak trees. At first the route may not be clear, but look out for yellow waymarks painted on the far side of some of the oak trees as you pass them. A little further on, where the path climbs towards an embankment, its line becomes clearer.

From (5) the local walking circuit is signed left. It climbs up into the hills ahead, turns back, clockwise, and returns to this point down the path on your right.

Looking north down the Ariège valley, from a viewpoint above Pitot on the long walk

Emerge onto a farm track (8), with a farmstead (Pitot) below right. Turn left onto the track; it immediately turns sharp right. You now begin a long, hard climb of the steep scarp that you have been approaching since the start of the walk. The track zigzags up the hillside, passing close to several curiously shaped outcrops of limestone. ◀

The track finally reaches the crest of a ridge, where it turns sharp right. However, it is well worth the extra effort to first of all turn left and follow an unwaymarked path which runs along the ridge. After only a minute or so the ridge drops away sharply and you enjoy a splendid view (9) – one of the best on this walk – towards Foix and its surrounding hills and mountains. On the next stage you will be heading for the bulky ridge, close by on the right.

Return to the waymarked track. It terraces, slightly to the left of the ridgeline. Be especially careful to pick up the next turning, which arrives very soon at a point where a fence (left) turns left and goes steeply downhill. There is a yellow waymark arrow on a rock on the right (pointing in the direction you have just come). Here you turn left and follow the fence down the slope (which may be muddy and slippery in wet weather).

You reach a meadow in the bottom of a valley. Continue for a short distance up the slope ahead, then go through a gate on the left. The next section of this walk, although waymarked, can be tricky to follow, so take particular care. The path enters woodland and traverses the hillside, then enters semi-open country. The ridge over on the left with the rocky, irregular spine is the one from which, a short while ago, you had the 'splendid view... towards Foix'.

The path you are now on passes strangely shaped crags and boulders. It suddenly turns right and climbs the hillside very steeply. In due course it reaches a small col with a huge rock outcrop on the left, then descends into the low woodland beyond, and continues the hill-side traverse.

After a short scramble up a steep embankment, emerge at the far end of a rough jeep track (10).

The uncultivated semi-open ground here is rich in wildlife and you may see a wide variety of wild flowers as well as birds of prey hovering and swooping overhead.

Route-finding from here on is generally much simpler. Go straight ahead along the track. This also traverses the hillside, and at first goes downhill a little. You are now in fairly open country, so once again the views are extensive and impressive.

You will see occasional yellow waymarks on the rock on the right of this track. But when the track turns around the second of two spurs (11), the waymarked trail actually goes over a fence on the left and starts a steep descent of the hillside. Leave that waymarked circuit here and keep to the jeep track straight ahead.

The track, now unwaymarked, is quite long and, later, climbs a little. Eventually it turns to the right, enters woodland and immediately reaches the col de Porte Pa (12). You may have to cross a wire fence here. If so, cross with care, because the fence is serving the admirable purpose of keeping motor vehicles off the track you have just walked along.

At the col you meet the Sentier Cathare, going from right to left, indicated with red and yellow waymarks. Turn left, go through a gate, and follow the Sentier Cathare all the way into Foix. It winds up the steep slope ahead, but take comfort from the fact that this is the last serious climb on the walk (unless you later plan to visit Foix castle, which sits on a hill overlooking the town).

Towards the upper part of the climb, you emerge into open country again. The trail ahead runs to the left of the crest of the ridge you are on, with fabulous views across to the Ariège mountains.

Where the slope levels out and the track forks, go right. This takes you to the right of the ridge crest, with views now to the north over the outer foothills of the Pyrenees and, beyond, to the flatter country extending to Castelnaudry and Toulouse.

Pass to the right of the highest point of the ridge – the Pech de Foix. That point, however, is surrounded by trees and has no views. Near where the crest of the ridge comes down on the left to join your track, there is a superb view on the right over the Ariège river (widened at one point by a barrage) and beyond to the cathedral town of Pamiers.

The Sentier Cathare descends a little to the left, crossing the crest of the ridge. Where the track swings to the right, and goes through a line of trees, take the path which branches off sharply to the left (ignoring another path which goes downhill straight ahead) (13). You may see a homemade sign on a tree pointing towards Foix. If so, that confirms the direction you should be taking.

The path, now in semi-woodland, descends to the right. You soon reach the top corner of a sizeable, but ruined, stone-built farmstead (the Pech de Naut). Your path goes across the open ground in front of the ruins, down a short embankment, then turns to go half-right. The line of the path may be a little obscure, but soon becomes clear again.

The trail traverses and gently descends the slope of the hill ahead. Meet an access track coming down on the right at a sharp bend in that track. Go straight ahead there, still descending. The outer reaches of Foix and the Ariège river are down on the left; directly behind you can see Montgaillard and the 'Sugar Loaf'.

Come to a corner of a fence, enclosing a field below left. Your route goes to the half-right, again downhill. The path enters semi-woodland and goes under a power line.

Keep an eye open now for a well-used but unway-marked path which forks off to the left (14), just before the Sentier Cathare turns distinctly to the right and where, a few metres on the right, there is an pylon along the power line. That path takes you along a rocky spur of land, wooded at first, then open. It leads to another very fine viewpoint, from where there is a superlative panorama over Foix, its castle, and the hills surrounding the town.

Return to the Sentier Cathare and turn left along it. It turns sharp right, then sharp left. The path becomes quite stony and descends more steeply, bending to the right as it does so. Mostly enclosed by woodland, it passes through a wooden gate and continues to wind downhill. As you begin to approach the foot of the hill, you will see Foix railway station down on the right. Eventually you come to a point where the path forks (15). The Sentier Cathare goes right, but the unway-marked path to the left offers a more exciting (and shorter) final descent into Foix, so take that.

After a steep descent, the path suddenly emerges above gardens and houses just above the Ariège river. Foix lies on the other side of the river, and soaring above the town is the immense, three-towered castle of Foix. The path winds down past the houses and, indeed, underneath them, to come out on a main road which runs alongside the river and railway line at a point almost directly opposite the Pont Vieux.

Cross that bridge, and walk through the town, up to Foix castle (16).

ROUTE DESCRIPTION – SHORT WALK

Distance:	8km (5 miles)
Time:	3hr
Altitude:	370m to 850m
Map:	as for long walk

This walk begins below **Foix castle** (16). Walk down through the **old town** to the Pont Vieux. This bridge links the old town to the main road along the east bank of the River Ariège.

Cross the bridge and turn left along the main road. The river and the railway line are immediately below left, with the town and castle rising up on the other side. Just before reaching a road on the left (which comes up from the railway station), cross the main road and go right up the rue Sainte Rapine. At the start of that road is the first signpost for the Sentier Cathare.

After about 250m turn right, down a lane, and at the end of that lane turn right, onto a footpath going up into woodland. The trail begins a long, steep climb. It passes through a wooden gate, then goes left at a path fork (15). Later, it passes through another small gate. Having swung to the left, the path suddenly turns sharply to the right.

Keep an eye open now for a well-used but unway-marked path which forks off to the right (14) where, a few metres on the left, there is a pylon along a power line. That path will take you along a rocky spur of land, wooded at first, then open. It leads to a very fine view-point, from where there is a superlative panorama over Foix, its castle, and the hills surrounding the town. Then return to the Sentier Cathare and turn right, along it.

The slope becomes less steep, the woodland thins out and you go under a power line. The trail then bears to the half-left, towards the top corner of a fence enclosing a field ahead. Pass to the left of that fence corner and follow the path as it traverses the semi-open hillside. Where a track turns off, sharp left, continue on the path straight ahead.

You then approach, on the half-left, a sizeable, but ruined, stone-built farmstead (marked on the IGN 1:25,000 map as the Pech de Naut). Climb towards those ruins and pass to the right-hand side of them. Follow the path beyond them straight up the slope through semi-woodland. Higher up, bear left.

Emerging into more open country near the top of the ridge, meet a track coming through a line of trees on the left (13). Turn right onto that track and follow it over the crest of the ridge. Ignore a track that forks to the right to go along the ridge. Follow the trail as it bears right and runs parallel to the ridge, with the higher ground now on your right. The highest point on the ridge – the Pech de Foix (860m) – is surrounded by trees and has no views. To the left are views over the outer foothills of the Pyrenees and, beyond, to the flatter country extending to Castelnaudry and Toulouse.

Further on the track crosses to the right-hand side of the ridge, from where you have fabulous views across to the Ariège mountains. Turn round and follow your outward route back to Foix.

When you reach the path fork at point (15) on the way back, turn left instead of right. Follow the route as described from that point in the description for the long walk, above.

POINTS OF INTEREST

Ariège valley: This wide, handsome valley is a principal artery of communication between the plains to the north – in which lie Pamiers and Toulouse – and the high mountains and Spain to the south. This is where the Cathar church in 13th-century Languedoc had its strongest following. Its followers escaped up the valley, heading for the Pyrenean cols which led them away from their French persecutors. There are many places of interest in and around the valley, including Ax-les-Thermes, a spa town which is an excellent base for walking in the Ariège mountains and for exploring other Cathar sites in Ariège.

Foix castle and museum: The solid, three-towered castle of Foix sits on a vertical-sided rock outcrop. It offers today one of the most powerful and well-known images of Cathar castle country. From the castle's high battlements there is a glorious view over Foix and up the Ariège valley. Inside is a departmental museum, devoted mainly to archaeology and military history. The castle and museum are open to the public on most days throughout the year.

Foix town centre: The narrow streets and crowded buildings in the centre of Foix, below the castle, testify to the town's medieval origin. There are several attractive timber-framed houses, fountains and squares. The oldest and probably the most interesting of all the streets in the old town is rue des Grands Ducs, just below and to the south of the castle. The overhead passages linking buildings on either side are especially impressive. To the north of the castle, and close to the river, is St-Volusien church. Its spacious, elegant, simple interior is well worth admiring. There was once a powerful abbey here.

Visiting times

Allow 2hr to have a good look around Foix castle and museum. A stroll around Foix town centre, visiting the various squares, churches and other interesting buildings, would take at least 2hr. Add shopping time, according to taste.

Rock formation above Pitot, on the long walk

Further information

- Office de Tourisme du Pays de Foix: 29, rue Delcassé, BP 20, 09001 Foix; tel: (00 33) (0)5 61 65 12 12; foix.tourisme@wanadoo.fr; **www.ot-foix.fr**.
- Foix castle and museum: tel: (00 33) (0)5 61 65 56 05.
- The local walking circuits followed by the first part of the long walk are nos 7 and 8 in an FFRP *Topo-guide, Le Pays de Foix à pied* (9 Euros). This is available in local shops and from the Comité Départemental Ariègeois de Randonnée Pédestre, 26 Fbg Planissolles, 09000 Foix; cdrp.09@wanadoo.fr; **http://perso.wanadoo.fr/cdrp.09/accueil.htm**. It also offers fascinating and well-illustrated information about the countryside around Foix, wildlife, history, legends, and so on.
- No 10 in that *Topo-guide* is the short walk, from Foix up to near the Pech de Foix and back.
- If you are using Foix as a base from which to explore the Ariège valley and its surrounding area, useful information can be obtained from the Comité Départemental du Tourisme Ariège Pyrénées, 31 bis avenue du Général de Gaulle, BP 143, 09000 Foix; tel: (00 33) (0)5 61 02 30 70; **www.ariegepyrenees.com**.

5 ROQUEFIXADE

One walk, modest in length but of very fine quality, is described in this section.

The walk starts and finishes in Roquefixade village, below the castle. It follows waymarked paths alongside meadows with abundant wild flowers, descends through a superb beech forest, then climbs back to higher ground. On the final section, you suddenly emerge onto a steep-sloping, open hillside above Roquefixade castle. From here there are far-reaching and striking views to the high Ariège mountains, rising to over 3000m. The sight of Roquefixade castle from this final stretch is breathtaking – one of the best panoramas in Cathar castle country.

CATHAR HISTORY: APRIL 1229

The scant but enormously impressive remains of Roquefixade castle are perched on one of the most awe-inspiring locations in the Cathar country.

Roquefixade castle was a stronghold of Cathar society in the early 13th century. In 1200 Raymond de Péreille, from a leading Cathar family, was married there. He later became lord of nearby Montségur.

After Simon de Montfort was killed in 1218, the crusade was driven back and the Cathars regained strength. But in 1226 the King of France, Louis VIII, relaunched the crusade. He did so with a single-mindedness unrecognised in his predecessors, and with an army so strong it was clear victory was inevitable.

The result was almost complete capitulation by the lords of Languedoc. In April 1229 the Count of Toulouse signed the Treaty of Paris with the French Crown, leading to the incorporation of Languedoc in the French kingdom. French forces quickly took control of most of the region.

Paradoxically, perhaps, Roquefixade played no significant role during the crusade, but it lay in the mountain country to which significant numbers of Cathars hastily retreated after the Treaty of Paris was signed. Leaders and followers of the Cathar faith fled in particular to Montségur, and many of them must have passed Roquefixade on their journey.

Later events
Later in the 13th century the French crown took over Roquefixade castle

and installed a garrison there. In 1632 the French king ordered it to be demolished, and this was done with meticulous care. The castle's remains have been crumbling into ruin ever since.

PRACTICAL INFORMATION
Access to starting point
Roquefixade is about 12km east of Foix. By road, take the N20 from Foix going south down the Ariège valley, then turn east onto the D117 heading for Lavelanet. Roquefixade lies to the north of that road; watch for signs directing you off the D117 towards Roquefixade castle. There is a small space for parking motor vehicles in the southwest corner of the village, alongside the D9a road.

Public transport in this area is scarce, although there are some buses running between Foix and Lavelanet that would take you to within a couple of kilometres of Roquefixade.

Navigation
Red and yellow waymarks show the route from its start in Roquefixade village (1) to near Coulzonne (3), and

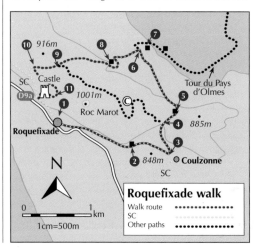

from near Bac-d'en-haut (7) to Roquefixade. Yellow waymarks denote the route for most of the rest of the circuit. Wherever there are red and yellow waymarks, you are on the Tour du Pays d'Olmes. You also follow the Sentier Cathare from points (1) to (3) and (10) to (1).

The path between points (5) and (6), a long descent through beech forest, was not shown on the 2000 edition of the 1:25,000 map. However, it is well used, carries yellow waymarks, and is easy to follow.

Roquefixade castle: one of the most spectacular locations in Cathar castle country. In the far distance are the Ariège mountains.

ROUTE DESCRIPTION

Distance:	8km (5 miles)
Time:	3hr
Altitude:	620m to 950m
Map:	IGN 2147ET (Foix Tarascon-sur-Ariège); Roquefixade is in map fold 4D

From the square in **Roquefixade village** (1), go to the left of the church, then take a turning on the left and meet the lane which runs along the back of the village. Turn right along that lane. It soon becomes a grass track, leading away from the village in a roughly eastward direction.

The track climbs a little, then terraces along the side of the hill. The crags below Roc Marot are on your left, with lower ground on the right. The St-Barthélemy mountains rise majestically beyond the lower ground. You may catch glimpses of the steep-sided hill on which sits Montségur castle, almost straight ahead.

From (3) walk a few metres straight ahead to the hamlet of Coulzonne; the old buildings and view towards Montségur are worth admiring. Retrace your steps and turn right down the track.

The path passes the **Resistance memorial** (2), in a peaceful patch of open ground with a couple of benches. The track then swings to the left of a hill, with a small, open valley on the left. Another grass track coming up on the left joins your track by a footpath signpost. The route turns sharp left down that track (3). ◀

You will soon see yellow waymarks alongside the grass track, which swings to the right then reaches another signposted path junction (4). Here, our route lies straight ahead, but an alternative route (also with yellow waymarks and signposted for Roquefixade) goes down to the left.

The alternative path later passes to the left of a large and impressive cave which plunges steeply into the hillside (the Grotte de l'église catholique). It rejoins the walk at point (9).

From point (4), continue straight ahead, signposted for Grézat and Ilhat. The track turns to the left, crosses some boulders lying near the ruins of Grézat, enters woodland, then turns again to the left (5).

Go straight ahead from (6), turn right at the next path crossing, to reach more open terrain by a fine old building – Bac-d'en-haut (7); glimpses of lower hill country to the north. Return to the main route.

The path (yellow waymarks), now descends for a considerable distance in a northwesterly direction. The whole descent runs through a splendid stretch of woodland, consisting predominantly of very fine beech trees.

Near the bottom of the slope you reach a path crossing (6). You route lies to the left, up a wide path which climbs steeply through the woodland, followed by the Tour du Pays d'Olmes. ◀

Start to tackle the long climb through the woodland, on the path now carrying red and yellow waymarks. In

due course, the path swings sharply to the left, then soon after turns right. Not long after watch out for a small path going off right; 50m along it you will find a fine *orri* (a drystone cabin) (8).

The orri on the Roquefixade walk

The slope of the main route now eases and the country around becomes semi-open. The alternative route (see above) joins from the left (9).

Finally, emerge onto the western end of the ridge coming down from Roc Marot – and the landscape changes suddenly and dramatically (10). In the far distance ahead are the high mountains of Ariège; to the left is the imposing massif of St-Barthélemy; also to your left, but much closer, is the precipitous blade of limestone on which are perched the scant but striking remains of **Roquefixade castle**.

The waymarked route follows the track downhill to your right. That track does a sharp turn to the left, then meets the Sentier Cathare which comes in on the right. It continues straight ahead, and descends into Roquefixade village (1).

Assuming you wish to visit the castle remains, and to approach them by the most impressive route from point (10), proceed from there as follows. Turn left off the waymarked route onto a path, which roughly follows the line of the ridge on your left. It is well trodden, with no signs saying that you are on forbidden land.

The path goes to the right of one rock outcrop, then to the left of another, then emerges onto an open grass slope. Roquefixade castle is on your right, on the other side of a steeply plunging short valley. Contour across the grass slope until you reach the far end of the hill, near the head of the short valley. From there (11), you can see the rusty-red roofs of Roquefixade village immediately below.

The castle remains are now accessible across a narrow neck of land on your right.

To go down to the village from the castle, follow the path descending the steeply plunging valley beneath and to the right of the castle, then turn left onto the track at the bottom. Pass immediately below the crag on which the castle sits. The track soon leads into the village at its top western corner (1).

POINTS OF INTEREST

Roquefixade village: In contrast to most medieval villages – which cluster in irregular fashion around a church – Roquefixade village was created from scratch, hence its rectilinear plan. This was done in the 13th century after the crusade, as the French kingdom consolidated its hold on the territory.

Memorial to French Resistance fighters: At point (2) you pass a memorial erected to 16 local members of the French Resistance who were killed during an attack by 400 German troops and French militia on nearby Coulzonne. It took place shortly before the liberation, on 6 July 1944.

Orri: Ingenious, age-old, drystone constructions found in various forms throughout the Mediterranean region of France and used for centuries for shelter and/or storage. *Orris* in the mountains were used until relatively recently by shepherds when they brought their livestock up to the high pastures for summer grazing. The *orri* at (8) is said to be linked to former charcoal-making activity in the forest.

Roquefixade castle: The remains may be scant, but they occupy one of the most impressive positions in the whole region. Access to the site is unobstructed and free but, as a notice in the village says, the castle is a '*site vertigineux*' and should be approached with '*prudence*'.

Looking back towards the castle at the end of the walk

Visiting time

Allow about 1hr for exploring Roquefixade castle and for savouring the five-star views from the hillside overlooking the castle.

Further information

- This walk is based on (though not exactly the same as) one in *Topo-guide, Pays d'Olmes*, published by the Communauté de Communes Pays d'Olmes (see below), price 2 Euros (2004). The booklet covers several other walks, including one to the summit of the Pic de St-Barthélemy, described in section 9 Montségur.
- Communauté de Communes Pays d'Olmes: 32 rue Jean Jaurès, 09300 Lavelanet; tel: (00 33) (0)5 34 09 33 80; tourisme@paysdolmes.org; **wwwpaysdolmes.org**.
- Lavelanet tourist office (stocks the above booklet): Maison de Lavelanet, BP 89 - 09300 Lavelanet; tel: (00 33) (0)5 61 01 22 20; lave anet.tourisme@wanadoo.fr.

6 LORDAT

Two walks are recommended in this section. The Lordat castle walk is circular, and though demanding is not long. It follows delightful local paths connecting villages on the impressive slopes of the Ariège valley. Lordat castle towers over most of the route.

The Lordat mountain walk is a fairly long, out-and-back route which climbs into the St-Barthélemy mountain range, north of Lordat. The walk passes close to the most beautiful of all the lakes in Cathar castle country, the Etang d'Appy.

Note: You may be tempted to climb the Pic de St-Barthélemy (2348m). It is possible to do that, from Appy village, via the Jasse de Sédars and the col de Girabel. However, it is a very strenuous mountain walk on a poorly waymarked route. It is outside the range of this book and should only be tackled by experienced mountain walkers. A better-waymarked and slightly less taxing route to the summit, from the north, is described in section 9 Montségur.

CATHAR HISTORY: JUNE 1229

The remains of Lordat castle are perched 400m above the Ariège valley. Much higher still, to the north of Lordat, are the St-Barthélemy mountains. Ancient routes through mountain passes lead down to Montségur, to the north. Lordat castle – parts of which date back to the 10th century – occupied a strategic position, guarding access to high passes leading into Spain.

Lordat and the surrounding mountainous country were hardly touched by the crusaders' armies, even though the Cathar church enjoyed strong support there. Lordat has been described as a 'Cathar village' and, until well into the 13th century, many Cathar sympathisers lived in the village or nearby. There is evidence of a Cathar cemetery close to Lordat.

But the fate of the people of Lordat was determined by the outcome of the crusade. Following the Treaty of Paris, the then Count of Foix submitted to the King of France. As a pledge of good faith, he had to hand over some of his castles for a period of five years. One of those was Lordat, which passed temporarily to the French Crown in June 1229.

Later events

A campaign of brutal and systematic suppression of the Cathar church throughout Languedoc followed the Treaty of Paris. It eventually led to the Cathar church being completely crushed. But this process took longest in remoter mountain locations like Lordat. Indeed, after the fall of Montségur in 1244, Lordat probably became for a while one of the most important Cathar centres.

Lordat played a role in a resurgence of the Cathar church in the early 14th century, led by Pierre Authié, by profession a *notaire* (lawyer) based in nearby Ax. One of Authié's followers was his son-in-law Arnaud Teisseyre, who lived in Lordat. Teisseyre gave Authié refuge there when the latter went into hiding.

The castle was strengthened by the French in the 14th century, but thereafter its military significance declined and it began to fall into ruin. Today, the striking hilltop castle is being developed as a tourist resource, with flying displays by eagles and other birds of prey within the castle walls.

Looking down on Lordat village and the hills beyond, from inside Lordat castle

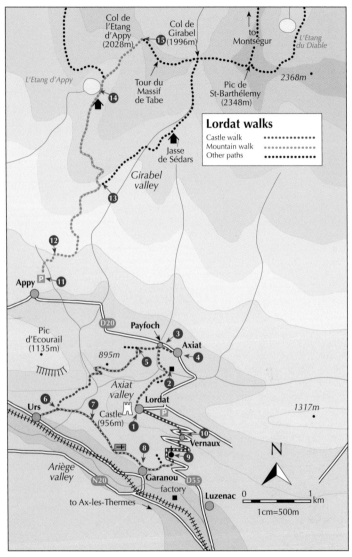

Col de
l'Etang
d'Appy
(2028m) — 15

Col de
Girabel
(1996m)

to
Montségur

*L'Etang
du Diable*

L'Etang d'Appy

14

2368m

Tour du
Massif
de Tabe

Pic de
St-Barthélemy
(2348m)

Jasse
de Sédars

*Girabel
valley*

13

Lordat walks

Castle walk ••••••••••
Mountain walk ••••••••••
Other paths ••••••••••

12

Appy P — 11

Pic
d'Ecourail
(1135m)

D20

Payfoch 3

Axiat 4

895m

5

2

*Axiat
valley*

6
Urs

7

Lordat P

1

Castle
(956m)

1317m

10

Vernaux

8

9

*Ariège
valley*

N20

Garanou

D55

factory

Luzenac

to Ax-les-Thermes

N

0   1 km

1cm=500m

PRACTICAL INFORMATION
Access to starting points
There are rail and bus services running along the Ariège valley; it would be possible to start and finish the Lordat walk at Garanou or Urs, visiting Lordat castle en route. Otherwise, public transport in this area is scarce.

To reach Lordat by road, from the N20 main road through the Ariège valley, take the turning for Luzenac and follow signposts for Lordat castle up the winding D55. Parking in Lordat village is very limited, but there is space for vehicles a short distance above the village at the junction of the D20 and D55 (picnic tables, drinking fountain, and fabulous views over the Ariège valley and forests and mountains beyond.) From that car park, walk back down to and through the village to the foot of the castle, for the Lordat castle walk.

To reach the village of Appy (for the Lordat mountain walk), follow the D20 from above Lordat, through Axiat and along to Appy. Follow signposts to a car park above the village. But beware: the route to the car park goes up very narrow, twisting village streets – too narrow, perhaps, for large vehicles and cars with caravans. The Lordat mountain walk, to l'étang d'Appy, is signposted from that car park.

Navigation
The route of the Lordat castle walk is indicated by yellow waymarks and signposts carrying the number 9 (as designated in a local guidebook). Signs for other waymarked walks, with other numbers, will be seen en route. Don't be lured in the wrong direction.

The route of the Lordat mountain walk is indicated by red waymarks and signposts carrying the number 24 (this walk's number in another local guidebook). There are traces of former yellow waymarks on the route, but these should be ignored.

Note: Waymarks on the climb from Appy to the Pic de St-Barthélemy are many and various, but are also almost completely absent along certain sections of the walk. Don't attempt this walk unless you feel confident that you can find your way using map and compass only.

ROUTE DESCRIPTION – LORDAT CASTLE WALK

Distance:	10km (6.2 miles)
Time:	3hr
Altitude:	590m to 900m
Map:	IGN 1:25,000 2148ET (Ax-les-Thermes); Lordat is in map fold 5B

In Lordat village (1) – with, on your left, a track which passes a ticket office and climbs to **Lordat castle** – take the grass track which leads north away from the village, in the direction of the mountain beyond. At first, this shady track descends gradually, past semi-wooded meadows.

Where the track forks, go right, then immediately fork left again. Not long after turn left off the track onto a stony path which descends steeply through woodland into the valley below.

On reaching a mountain stream (which, like most others on this walk, starts high up on the slopes of the Pic de St-Barthélemy), cross over by an old stone bridge (2). Immediately opposite are the remains of a former mill. Beyond the stream, follow the path to the left as it climbs the other side of the valley (possibly quite wet underfoot).

Eventually the path meets the D20 road in the village of Payfoch (3). The route of the walk goes left here. ◀

Go along the D20 road for a few metres then, by another mountain stream, turn left off the road down a lane which very soon bears to the right. The lane passes the backs of some stone-built houses, almost at roof level. At a lane intersection, turn left. That lane descends steeply through the village, bears right and passes to the right of a large modern barn. It becomes an unsurfaced farm track, with woodland on the left.

From (3) turn right along the road into Axiat to admire the superb Romanesque church (4) at the far end. As you approach Axiat, Lordat castle can be seen right. Return to Payfoch.

Just before the track reaches open country, turn onto a path descending to the left alongside woodland (5). This path soon emerges into completely open country and swings to the right. It becomes a magnificent pedestrian's corniche, one of the most beautiful paths in this book. It terraces high above the Axiat valley, immediately below on the left. There is often a great profusion of colourful wild flowers alongside the path. The remains of Lordat castle can be seen looming high above the other side of the valley; straight ahead is a gigantic cliff face below the Pic d'Écourail. Way below, on the half-left in the Ariège valley, is the village of Urs, this path's destination.

In due course the path starts to wind down the valley side. It enters woodland and crosses a tributary stream plunging into the Axiat valley. The path climbs a little, bears to the right, re-enters open country, then descends past hay meadows towards the village of Urs.

Just before the path reaches the village, it meets a grass track (6). The route turns left here, along the track. ▶

Continue east along the grass track heading away from Urs. That track crosses the Axiat river by a substantial wooden footbridge, then climbs into woodland. Fork

From (6) a short diversion (right) leads to Urs village and imposing church, located on the other side of the Ariège valley railway line linking Toulouse and Barcelona. Return to (6).

The exquisite 11th-century church of Sainte-Marthe, on the Lordat castle walk

right onto a path which climbs more steeply; go right again on meeting another track. After a further short climb, emerge into an open area with an old quarry wall on the left and an access track immediately ahead (7). Go along that access track.

Once more in open country, pass a cemetery on the left, then enter the village of Garanou (8). The village washing-place on the left is very pretty. Keep to the left as you go through the village. Take a road bearing uphill to the left. The wide, strong-flowing Ariège river is not far below on the right. So is a huge factory which processes talc, brought down by cable car from a quarry high on the mountainside.

Ignoring the rue du Château on the left, go up to a road intersection and turn right. Very soon afterwards take a grass path forking up to the left. This brings you onto the D55; turn sharp left along that road. You now have a long, fairly steep climb back to Lordat. Fortunately there are a number of cool water fountains on the way, especially in the next village, Vernaux.

Falcons, eagles and vultures put on a flying display from inside Lordat castle

The road bends to the right and you reach the 11th-century church of Sainte-Marthe (9), its charm and delicacy accentuated by its tiny windows and the heavily weathered nature of the stone used in its construction.

Continue to follow the road as it turns right and, later, turns sharp left. Further along, turn sharp right onto a lane with a 'no entry' sign for motor vehicles. You enter Vernaux (10). Bear to the left, then to the right through the village, passing the *mairie* on your right. On reaching again the D55, turn left along that road for a few metres, then go right, up another steep lane through the village. On meeting the road again, go straight across and climb up the grass track opposite. That track once again crosses the road and by now you have left the village.

After a long, steady climb, meet a farm track at a bend in that track. Go straight ahead, up that track. It bends right and soon meets the road. Turn left along the road. After not too long, re-enter Lordat village (1). The view of the castle from here is striking and, if you look down to the left, you can see the church of Sainte-Marthe, passed earlier on.

ROUTE DESCRIPTION – LORDAT MOUNTAIN WALK

Distance:	12km (7.4 miles)
Time:	5hr
Altitude:	980m to 2028m
Map:	as for Lordat castle walk; Appy is also in map fold 5B

From the car park above Appy village (11), follow a well-used path signposted for l'étang d'Appy which heads north up the side of the mountain. The path is clear and mostly obvious, but keep an eye on the waymarks; paths created by grazing livestock occasionally go off left and right – do not wander off on one of these.

Shortly after passing under a power line, turn right at path fork (12) (the left fork goes to a climbing cliff). After passing under a second power line, the path crosses a broad ridge and climbs steadily, high above the Girabel river, now far down on the right.

Eventually the path forks (13). Turn sharp left, uphill here. The path then zigzags steeply uphill along the edge of a partly burnt area of woodland. You pass a source of water – the flow of water may be feeble, but it is worth noting. ▶

From (13) go straight on for the direct route to the Pic de St-Barthélemy – see above.

The path climbs steadily northwestwards, then reaches and crosses a broad but rocky ridge at 1680m. From almost the start to this point, there has been a fine view back towards **Lordat castle**. On the other side of the ridge the path gradient eases considerably and you even drop down a little.

The terrain becomes wilder and more irregular. Eventually, at the top of a gentle rise, the wonderful Etang d'Appy, in its enormous glaciated mountain basin, suddenly comes into view just below. A cabin on the right, with a corrugated iron roof, is open and can be used as shelter during storms. Drop down to the lakeside (14); the red waymarks end here.

Now take an unwaymarked but broad and very well-used path which zigzags steadily up the slope on your right, towards the col de l'Etang d'Appy. In clear weather, the col can easily be seen high above the lake. Once at the col (15) you are on the main crest of this range of mountains. There is an immense view to the north across the foothills of the Pyrenees out to the plain between Carcassonne and Toulouse; beyond that you may also be able to see the Montagne Noire. To the south and west are the serrated peaks and ridges of the Pyrenees, rising high above the Ariège valley.

Return to Appy by the same route.

A jewel in the mountains: the Etang d'Appy, above Lordat

From the col de l'Etang d'Appy, the Tour du Massif de Tabe follows the main west–east ridge all the way to the Pic de St-Barthélemy. If you are tempted to follow it, bear in mind that it is a mountain scramble with a steep, exposed descent over loose, stony ground, followed by a very long and steep climb. It too is outside the range of walks in this book and only suitable for experienced mountain walkers.

POINTS OF INTEREST

Lordat castle: See historical references at the start of this section. The castle is open most afternoons from April to November. Open every day during July and August, mornings and afternoons; one flying display in the morning, two in the afternoon. At other times one display only, in the afternoon. At the time of writing entry fee is 6 Euros; reductions for children and groups.

Visiting time
The remains of Lordat castle are interesting but not very extensive, but it is worth taking time to admire the views over the surrounding countryside, and for the display by the 'eagles of Lordat' (with a tour of the castle). Allow 2hr.

Further information
- The Lordat castle walk is no 9 in *Topo-guide 1 – d'un village à l'autre en Vallées d'Ax*. The Lordat mountain walk is no 24 in *Topo-guide 2 – Lacs & Torrents en Vallées d'Ax*. Both are excellent, inexpensive booklets (in French), produced by the Communauté de Communes des Vallées d'Ax. Available locally (see tourist offices below).
- Both walks are on the Internet (in French): go to **www.randonnees-ariege.com** and select walks in Pays de Foix-Haute Ariège.
- Ax-les-Thermes tourist office: 'La Résidence', 6 avenue Théophile Delcassé, 09110 Ax-les-Thermes, tel: (00 33) (0)5 61 64 60 60; vallees.ax@wanadoo.fr; **www.vallees-ax.com**.
- Luzenac tourist office (the nearest one to Lordat): 6, rue de la mairie, 09250 Luzenac.
- A locally available booklet in French, *Lordat – château fuxéen, village cathare*, by Gabriel de Llobet (1995) has fascinating information about the history of Lordat castle and village.

7 MONTAILLOU

The circuit described in this section is a first-class full-day hill walk, mostly in open country surrounded by higher mountains. It passes through Montaillou village, climbs to a ridge from where there are magnificent views towards the Ariège mountains in particular, then traverses that ridge before descending to the starting point.

Montaillou castle is visible from many parts of the walk. At 1354m, it is the highest of all the Cathar castles focused on in this book.

CATHAR HISTORY: 1233

Montaillou, a small village with unassuming castle remains, is tucked away in hills northeast of Ax-les-Thermes. It is inextricably linked to the Inquisition, which began in 1233.

Although Simon de Montfort burned, slaughtered and mutilated thousands of Cathars. Many people, especially in the mountainous areas, clung to the Cathar faith. The Catholic Church realised that it needed a much more effective instrument for eradicating the heresy. The instrument which it fashioned for that purpose was the Inquisition.

The Inquisition used imprisonment, terror and torture to extract confessions from Cathars. It divided families and communities by encouraging – indeed by requiring – neighbours and relatives to inform on those who were suspected of having Cathar sympathies. Like de Montfort, it burnt Cathars alive but, over a period of 100 years, the Inquisition in Languedoc committed far fewer people to the flames than de Montfort had done in less than a decade. Nevertheless, it proved to be a much more successful mechanism for wiping out the Cathar church.

Indeed, the Inquisition – created in Languedoc in 1233 – proved to be so efficient that it was applied throughout Europe and beyond to combat heresy and threats to the established order. As an institution, it survived for a further six centuries. Dictators worldwide employ its methods to this day.

The monks, priests and other men of the Church who conducted the Inquisition's hearings were meticulous. They kept detailed written records of their proceedings and of witnesses' statements and confessions. Surviving records have provided historians with their principal source of information about the Cathars.

Later events

Particularly rich are the recorded interrogations of the people of Montaillou. As late as the early 14th century, a majority of its inhabitants were still followers or sympathisers of the Cathar church. In 1308, at the time of the Cathar resurgence led by Authié (see Lordat, section 6), Montaillou was sealed off and its villagers arrested. Interrogations were held then, and again nine years later, under Jacques Fournier, who became Bishop of Pamiers in 1317.

It is what remains of the records of those interrogations which link Montaillou so closely to the Inquisition. Many of the hearings – which went on until 1324 – were conducted by Jacques Fournier. He later became Pope Benoît XII, taking the records with him for safekeeping. The records are famous not only because they tell historians a great deal about the Cathar faith and its church, but because they also provide a remarkably detailed account of the life of a medieval community in the mountains of Ariège.

Without doubt, the hero of that community was a walker – or, rather, a shepherd whose walking feats seem almost superhuman. He was a Cathar believer by the name of Pierre Maury. He moved his huge flocks of sheep hundreds of kilometres each year from their winter grazing grounds in Catalunya up to summer pastures at altitudes of around 2000m in the

Montaillou castle: the wild flowers in the foreground grow on the edge of the Cathars' former medieval village

Ariège and other parts of the Pyrenees. He stayed there for the whole summer, living with other shepherds in what may have been stone-built cabins similar to the *orris* which survive today (see Roquefixade, section 5). He joined a group of Ariège Cathars led by Bélibaste – the last of the Languedoc *Bons Hommes* – and which went into exile in Catalunya.

Maury was with Bélibaste when the latter was arrested in 1321, in a town not far south of present-day Andorra. Maury was not arrested and immediately went south on foot, covering nearly 200km in two days. He then walked from town to town, warning other Cathars of their leader's arrest and helping them to sell their possessions and move to places of greater safety. (Bélibaste was later burnt at the stake in Villerouge-Termenès – see section 14.)

As for the castle at Montaillou, its role was transformed in the mid-13th century from a seat of local power to a frontier fortress. The remains of the tower seen today probably date from that time. Like so many other castles hereabouts, Montaillou was totally abandoned in the 17th century and most of it subsequently demolished.

The medieval village was also abandoned and replaced by one lower down the hillside that we see today. Thanks to the Inquisition's records, historians know more about medieval life in Montaillou than any other village in Europe. One author (René Weis) has been able to reconstruct the precise layout of that village, with the names of the families who lived in every house in the early 14th century. Today, Montaillou is still the subject of detailed archaeological and historical studies.

PRACTICAL INFORMATION
Access to starting point

By road from Ax-les-Thermes, take the winding D613 that climbs to the col de Chioula. Beyond that col, the road descends to Prades, then Camurac. At Camurac, turn right towards a ski station. The start of this walk is a little way along that road on the right, by a tennis court. Camurac can also be approached from Quillan in the east (take the D117 towards Puivert, then soon turn left onto the D613 to Belcaire and Camurac).

Public transport in this area is scarce.

Navigation

You should carry the relevant IGN 1:25,000 map and a

compass for all the walks in this book, but for this one in particular it is essential.

The walk starts in the département of Aude, crosses into Ariège, then crosses back into Aude. Part of the route follows the GR7B and GR107 (Chemin des Bonshommes) long-distance paths, and you will encounter a considerable variety of waymarks and signposts.

At the very start in Camurac (1) is a sign carrying a yellow waymark indicating that you are on a walking route Les Crêtes. From there across to Montaillou (3) you follow an alternative loop of the GR7/GR107 connecting Comus, Camurac and Montaillou (red and white waymarks).

Between Montaillou (3) and the col de Balaguès (6) you are on the GR7B/GR107 (red and white waymarks). You will also see, near Montaillou castle, yellow waymarks for a local circuit; ignore these.

At the col de Balaguès the GR7B and the GR107 head off in different directions. From there you follow a local Ariège route (red waymarks and signposts). Those red signs, carrying the number 31, go as far as the Roc de Quercort (7) (and continue beyond, towards the Pic de Serembarre). At the Roc de Quercort you cross back into Aude and much of the rest of the route back down to Camurac is indicated with yellow waymarks and signposts.

Between the col de Balaguès (6) and the col de Teil (8) this walk roughly follows the crest of a broad, open ridge oriented approximately west–east. The line of the path along that ridge is not always clear. Don't depend on the waymarks (red at first, then yellow). Follow carefully the IGN 1:25,000 map – especially in mist. Take particular care not to bear off too much to the south (to your right). You could end up, puzzled, on the Pic Doulent, or find yourself striding purposefully, way off course, towards the Pic de Serembarre.

As you descend towards Camurac, the waymarked path (between about points [11] and [1]) may become overgrown. It is possible to follow a tarmacked road instead (below).

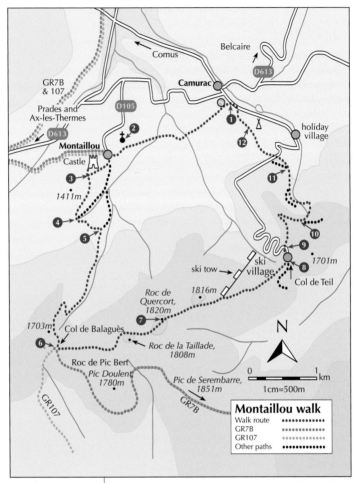

ROUTE DESCRIPTION

From the start (1), by the road that goes up to ski slopes just south of **Camurac**, follow the track that passes to the left of an enclosed tennis court. Go straight ahead where a lane on the right joins the track, and continue

Distance:	14km (8.7 miles)
Time:	6hr
Altitude:	1230m to 1820m
Map:	IGN 1:25,000 2148ET (Ax-les-Thermes) ; Montaillou is in map fold 10B

Note: If you haven't already done so, please read the notes on navigation above. They should be borne in mind at all times on this walk.

straight ahead again (that is, fork right) a few metres further along. You are now heading across some relatively level, open land towards the village of Montaillou, on a hill in the distance.

Keep to the main track across the lower ground ahead, ignoring other turnings. Some of the latter are signposted as a local mountain bike circuit. The track approaches and passes just to the left of a white church (2) just outside Montaillou. ▶

Climb up into **Montaillou village**. Just beyond the intersection with the D105 is an open space named after the French historian Emmanuel Le Roy Ladurie, a leading authority on the Cathars of Montaillou. Bear left

Several of the well-tended gravestones in the cemetery of the white church bear family names identical to some of those in the records of the Inquisition 700 years ago.

The present-day village of Montaillou – the Cathar medieval village lay higher up, above the slope on the right

at that intersection. You have now joined the GR7B; that route is also here followed by the GR107, the Chemin des Bonshommes.

Fork right and pass to the left of another church. The lane climbs fairly steeply through the village. Where the slope levels out just beyond the village, turn sharp right onto another track (3). This winds up the hill and soon brings you to the remains of **Montaillou castle**. The archaeological excavations of the medieval village are being carried out on the slope just beyond the castle.

From the castle, return to the track junction (3), and there turn right to follow the track that is signposted for the col de Balaguès. You immediately pass a spring on the right. The track traverses an open hillside and descends to a track crossing (4). A track going sharp left heads down a valley back to Montaillou.

Just to the right of the track going down to Montaillou, another one, which carries red and white waymarks (and which you should now take), climbs the wooded hillside opposite. This grass track winds over the hill, passing under a power line. You come to another track junction (5).

Turn right and follow the track that climbs the valley towards the higher ground. For most of the way, this track is out in the open, and makes for a hard climb on a hot day. Higher up it passes into shady woodland, but becomes even steeper for a while. Various other tracks leave the main one, so be careful to keep to the waymarked route.

The route meets and immediately crosses a forest track contouring around the valley. Shortly afterwards, emerge into the open, upper slopes of the hill. The path swings around to the right, then later turns sharp left. There follows a long traverse on a relatively gently incline towards the col de Balaguès, visible on the crest of the high ground ahead.

You finally reach the col de Balaguès (6). In clear weather you are suddenly greeted by one of the most magnificent mountain panoramas encountered anywhere in this book. From far left to far right, the high, serrated peaks and ridges of the Carlit and Ariège ranges fill the horizon.

Unless you have previously studied the various long-distance and local walking routes that branch off from this col, signposting and waymarking at this point will probably seem confusing. In essence, the GR107 heads south, the GR7B turns to the southeast, and a local circuit goes east along the ridge. You also want to go east along the ridge. The best policy for the time being is to ignore all path signposting and waymarking, and simply turn left at the col and climb the open shoulder of land ahead.

Pass to the right of a rocky outcrop, then bear very slightly to the left, to pass just to the left of the delightfully named Roc de Pic Bert. From here a reasonably well-defined path is indicated by low wooden stakes carrying red waymarks. Whether you are on that path or not, bear to the left, climb the hillside, then bear right, to pass just north of the Roc de la Taillade. If the highest point of this walk, the Roc de Quercourt (7), is now visible, the route to it will be obvious and you will reach it in about 5min. If visibility is poor, cross the flattish area of ground ahead in an east-northeast direction. You will soon come to a short steep slope, leading to a cairn on the top of the Roc de Quercourt.

On a clear day the view from this summit could be enjoyed for hours. Not only can you see a vast stretch of the Pyrenees to the south, you also have a very large part of Cathar castle country within range, including the Montagne Noire in the north and the Pic de Bugarach in the east. Montaillou, with the castle remains overlooking the village, lies immediately below. A little beyond Montaillou is Comus, on the Sentier Cathare. Rising high to the left of Comus is the white round dome of the Montagne de la Frau and the jagged Pic de Soularac, at the eastern end of the St-Barthélemy range.

From the Roc de Quercourt, the walk continues along the broad open ridge in an east-northeast direction. A route is now indicated by occasional yellow painted waymarks, but it is probably best to make your own way without worrying about waymarks. You may be able to see the top of a ski tow further along the ridge. If so, aim for that.

Pass to the right of the top of an unattractive ski tow. From here, descend to the left of the ridgeline, towards the col du Teil. There is a line of large wooden stakes going down to the col, and a grass track winding down to the right of those stakes. Around the col are several ski chalets.

At the col (8), turn left and follow a track passing through this ski village. Pass a car parking area below on the left, then meet a road coming up on the left. Turn right onto that road, but immediately – where that road swings sharp right (9) – go half-left onto a grass track contouring across the hillside ahead. A yellow path waymark a little way along that track indicates that you are on the correct route; watch out for similar waymarks all the way back to the start of the walk.

The track bears left into woodland, swings sharp right, then passes a metal road barrier to emerge into

The col de Balaguès (1669m). The Ariège mountains on the horizon rise to above 3000m.

open country again. You are at the head of a valley which plunges steeply to your left. Where the track forks, go down to the left (10). Pass under a ski tow and follow the track as it bears left around the head of the valley.

The track descends into forest and turns left. Shortly after re-emerging into open land after going under the ski tow again, fork right down a faintly defined track running along the edge of the forest, now on the right. Continue straight ahead where this track cuts off the main one, then soon meet the main track again, on the right. That track then re-enters woodland. The valley you have been descending is now falling away on your right.

As the track bears left, the waymarked route forks off to the right (11).

From (11) down to Camurac, sections of the waymarked route may be over-grown, especially in early summer. If you don't want to tackle this, simply keep to the track until it meets a tarmacked road. Turn right and follow the road as it winds downhill, through another holiday village and past a camp-site back to Camurac.

The waymarked path, after leaving the track, descends through the forest and soon meets the tarma-cked road. Turn left along that road for a very short distance, then turn off to the right to continue descending along the waymarked path. Go down through pine forest. The path bears to the right. It soon emerges into and crosses a short section of open ground and then meets a stony track.

Turn left along that track for a little way; there is a campsite on the right. Then turn left onto another path and follow that down to meet another track. Go left, but almost immediately turn right onto another path (12), which continues the descent towards Camurac. That path eventually emerges into an area of open ground. Cross that and very soon meet the tarmacked road again. Turn left onto the road and you almost immediately come down to the starting point (1).

POINTS OF INTEREST

Camurac is on the western margin of the Pays de Sault. A *pays* is a stretch of country in France with a distinctive geographical, and often cultural, personality. The Pays de Sault is an upland basin which stretches east towards (but does not go as far as) Quillan. Extensive sections are remarkably flat for such a high area.

Camurac lies – along with Montaillou, Comus and Prades – in a smaller and higher basin which has its own unique character and which is called the Pays d'Aillou (hence the name of the village, Montaillou).

Montaillou village and castle: See above (Cathar history).

Visiting time

Montaillou village and its castle remains are small, with no large exhibitions. The castle remains can be visited, but the archaeological site in the former village is not open to the public at present. So, if you allow 1hr to look around the present-day village and castle that will probably be more than ample.

Looking down on the present-day village of Montaillou, from the Roc de Quercort (1820m), the highest point on the walk. The remains of Montaillou castle sit on a terrace just above and to the left of the village.

Further information

- This is the *Camurac –Les Crêtes* walk, described in a locally available booklet published by the Office de Tourisme du Pays de Sault called *Pays de Sault – La Pleine Nature Atout Coeur!* (5 Euros).

- Office de Tourisme du Pays de Sault: Route d'Ax-les-Thermes, 11340 Belcaire; tel: (00 33) (0)4 68 20 75 89; o.t.p.s@wanadoo.fr.

- This walk is on the Internet at **www.paysdesault.com/rando_2_camurac.htm** – but this only gives the bare details. That website is a useful source of information about accommodation, places to eat, festivals and spectacles, and the history of various sites (including Montaillou) in this part of Cathar castle country.

- The highest part of this walk is followed by no 31 in *Topo-guide 2 – Lacs & Torrents en Vallées d'Ax*. The route just above Montaillou is also on that of a short walk based on Montaillou (no 22) described in *Topo-guide 1 – d'un village à l'autre en Vallées d'Ax*. Both are produced by the Communauté de Communes des Vallées d'Ax. They are available locally – for example, at Ax-les-Thermes tourist office: 'La Résidence', 6 avenue Théophile Delcassé, 09110 Ax-les-Thermes, tel: (00 33) (0)5 61 64 60 60; vallees.ax@wanadoo.fr; **www.vallees-ax.com**.

- The website at **www.mairie-montaillou.fr** is an excellent source of information about summer events in the village (historical reconstructions, conferences, etc), and about the archaeological work in Montaillou.

- Mairie de Montaillou: (00 33) (0)4 68 20 31 91.

- The FFRP's *Topo-guide* for the GR107 long-distance path, *Sur les traces des Cathare – Le Chemin des Bonshommes* contains interesting notes and photographs concerning Montaillou, Ax-les-Thermes, the Inquisition, the Ariège Cathars and their flight into Catalunya, etc. See Appendix 2.

- The classic work of reference on the medieval village is *Montaillou, village occitan de 1294 à 1324* by Emmanuel Le Roy Ladurie (Gallimard 1975, revised edition 1982). An English translation by Barbara Bray is entitled simply *Montaillou* (Penguin Books, 1978, reprinted 1990). Another, very readable, text in English is *The Yellow Cross, the story of the last Cathars 1209–1329* by René Weis (Viking 2000, Penguin Books 2001).

8 PUIVERT

Two circular walks from the village of Nébias, 5km southeast of Puivert castle, are described in this section. Puivert castle can be seen from various points along the way. The shorter walk goes to the north of Nébias, the longer goes to the south.

The shorter walk follows the route of a *Sentier Nature* ('nature trail'), also referred to as a *sentier de découverte* ('discovery path', or interpretation trail). It passes through some very unusual labyrinthine karst country – a wonderful natural maze.

The longer option follows a waymarked circular walk, part of which traverses forest-covered hills and part of which crosses a stretch of relatively level farmland occupied, until medieval times, by a huge lake. The outstanding feature is a superb *belvédère* (viewpoint) on a high cliff overlooking Puivert castle and Nébias.

CATHAR HISTORY: MAY 1242

The Inquisition was hated by most people in Languedoc. However, in 1242, the Count of Toulouse rebelled against the King of France. This rebellion proved fruitless but, while it lasted, it inspired certain Cathar soldiers who had taken refuge in Montségur to descend from their eagle's nest and strike at the Inquisition.

The event – a carefully planned massacre – took place in Avignonet, near Castelnaudry, on the night of 28 May 1242. Eleven officers of the Inquisition were lodging in the town. The vengeful Cathars slipped in and slaughtered them in their beds, then hurried back to Montségur before they could be intercepted.

One of the Cathars who took part was Gaillard de Congost. He was the son of Bernard de Congost, a Cathar who was formerly lord of Puivert and who died at Montségur in 1242. When they ruled at Puivert, the de Congost family made their castle a centre of Occitan culture. Troubadours and poets received a generous welcome. But the crusaders attacked the castle in November 1210 and took it after only three days of assault.

Legend has it that Bernard de Congost, with the young Gaillard in his arms, escaped from the castle by a secret underground tunnel only seconds before French soldiers burst into the room where they were taking refuge.

Whether that is true or not, it is easy to imagine that Gaillard de Congost was eager to take revenge on his family's oppressors, and that he needed little persuasion to take part in the Avignonet murders.

Puivert village

Later events
Most of the castle seen today was constructed by a wealthy French family in the early 14th century. Remains of the de Congost fortress are at the far western end.

Perhaps because it never presented any serious military threat, the castle was not systematically demolished. It suffered from neglect and pillage after the Revolution, but some restoration has been carried out more recently. This fortress is still one of the more substantial and imposing monuments in Cathar castle country.

PRACTICAL INFORMATION
Access to starting point
Nébias lies just to the north of the D117, which runs west from Quillan to Puivert, Lavelanet and Foix.

Public transport in this area is scarce.

Navigation
The Sentier Cathare, the GR7 long-distance path and various types of local walks, each with their own special waymarks, all converge on Nébias. Please note carefully the advice on waymarking at various points in the route descriptions.

The first part of the southern circular walk follows the Sentier Cathare south out of Nébias. The waymarks for that section – (1) to (11) – are blue and yellow. Then the route follows a local walk (yellow waymarks). That section – (11) to (15) – goes up to a fine *belvédère* (view-point), then descends. The third part of the walk, from the Lac de Tury back to Nébias – (15) to (1) – follows the GR7 (red and white waymarks).

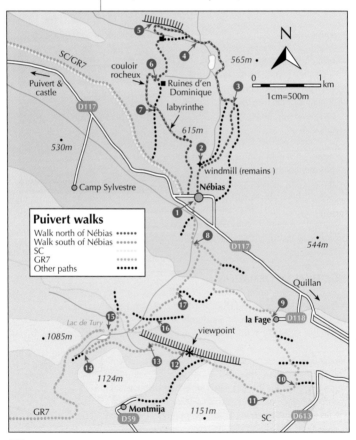

ROUTE DESCRIPTION – CIRCULAR WALK NORTH OF NÉBIAS

Distance:	8km (5 miles)
Time:	2.5hr
Altitude:	470m to 610m
Map:	IGN 1:25,000 2247OT (Lavelanet) and 2347OT (Quillan); Puivert is in map fold 8C of the Lavelanet map; Nébias is in map fold 10C of that map

From the square in the centre of **Nébias** (1), head west along the village's main street. On reaching the Chemin du Moulin à Vent on the right, turn up that lane. It climbs gently uphill, northwards, away from the village. You soon reach the restored remains of a stone-built windmill (2), with a small car park on the right. ▶

On the right is a large notice board giving information, in French, about a Sentier Nature. For the next 2.5hr or so you follow this circular trail, which is well used and extremely well signposted and waymarked (green painted arrows, small signs with the letters 'SN').

There are fine views from point (2); you can sit on the stones here and have a picnic lunch.

Looking down on Nébias from the belvédère on the southern Puivert walk

111

The trail at first crosses rough grazing fields, then enters dense woodland consisting mainly of box trees – almost ubiquitous in these parts.

After descending a fairly steep slope, the path meets a track where you turn left (3). Where the track forks a little further ahead, go right, and soon approach a lake in an open area. This is on the edge of a campsite and is private. The nature trail turns right, off the track, and follows a mown grass track across a meadow. On the other side of the meadow, climb and bear left, passing the lake now down below on your left.

After you have passed the lake, the track bears to the left and goes downhill through a relatively new plantation of conifers. At the bottom of the hill, turn sharp left where you meet another track, then soon after follow the signposts as they direct you to turn right.

The track winds downhill through woodland and crosses a small wooden footbridge over a streambed (4), then bears right and goes uphill. Crudely written notices, nailed to nearby trees, tell you that this is private property and that you must not shoot game or drive a motor vehicle.

Watch out for where the trail forks right, off the track, to follow a footpath which ascends to a ridge. Near the top the woodland thins out a little, and at the very top there is an open area with a steep cliff on your right (with chain-link fencing at its edge). There are fine views from here (5).

Follow the waymarked trail as it bears left, goes downhill, crosses another footbridge, and winds past a ruined, overgrown stone building on your right. The path forks here – take the left fork, emerge onto a

It really is easy to get lost in this natural limestone maze north of Nébias

LE LABYRINTHE

track almost immediately, turn right, then turn left at the track junction a few metres further ahead.

The track through the woodland now climbs steadily for a while. At the top it bears right and goes downhill to an open area. The path crosses this open area, winds in a curious fashion uphill on the other side, then turns sharp right where the half-hidden Ruines d'en Dominique can be seen opposite on the left, on the other side of a track (6).

After bearing left, then left again, the trail enters the *couloir rocheux* (the 'rocky passage'). This is the beginning of a remarkable goblins' grotto across a wooded, **limestone karst plateau**. As you squeeze along the winding channels worn into the limestone pavement, take care to follow the green arrows painted onto the rock; it is easy to lose your sense of direction in this enchanting and unusual place. Sometimes you enter a wide hollow in the rocks, and the limestone blocks seem like huge moss-covered toads, utterly still, but ready to pounce.

Sometimes the green arrows offer you a choice of route – which seems particularly confusing – but all the routes eventually rejoin. Other signposts indicate interesting features, such as standing stones or fine tree specimens. Among the latter the most striking is the *sapin harpe* – the 'harp-shaped fir tree' – with several vertical branches rising at regular intervals from its horizontal, ground-level trunk.

The nature trail meets the track you were lately walking on (7), and 'SN' signs tell you to turn left for a short distance along that track. Then you turn right, leaving the track. The maze of channels and hollows across the limestone plateau – here called *le labyrinthe* – continues and becomes even more bewildering.

Eventually the path ceases its bizarre activity, and you emerge onto open ground, which descends gently towards Nébias. Follow the trail across fields, passing to the right of the windmill remains. Follow the grass track ahead to the outskirts of Nébias and turn left on reaching the principal street through the village. You soon return to the starting point (1).

ROUTE DESCRIPTION – CIRCULAR WALK SOUTH OF NÉBIAS

Distance:	12km (7.4 miles)
Time:	5hr
Altitude:	560m to 1000m
Map:	as for circular walk north of Nébias

From the village square in the centre of **Nébias** (1) head south, passing to the right of the church.

Descend to the main road and cross that carefully. After crossing a stream, fork left. You are now in an open, almost flat area of farmland. At a track crossing go left (8). At another track crossing a little distance beyond, turn right. Go uphill along the edge of a field. At a track junction on the edge of a forest at the top of the field, turn left. This track terraces along a slope below cliffs high up on the right with an almost flat expanse of farmland (a **former lake**) below on the left.

Enter the hamlet of la Fage (9). Immediately turn right and skirt the western side of this settlement. Pass a fountain, on your right.

Leave the hamlet along a stony track heading towards the steep wooded slope straight ahead. At a track fork, go right. Start to climb more steeply. The track enters the forest, and swings to the left. In places, the track narrows and becomes quite stony. Meet a forest track: go straight across that. The long climb continues and the path zigzags uphill. Eventually the slope eases off, and you enter semi-open country.

Pass under a power line; then, on meeting a track (10), turn right along it. In due course your track bears to the left, at a point where it meets another jeep track coming across open ground on the right. You are now crossing semi-open farmland.

At this track junction (11), turn right onto the track going west across the open ground towards the forest-covered hill ahead. The track soon starts to climb into the forest. Keep to the waymarked track as it winds up the hill, and ignore other tracks forking off. Higher up, follow the waymarked route which cuts off bends followed by the track.

Eventually the slope levels out, and you approach open ground. Follow the waymarked path through a pine forest to the right, close to the edge of the open area. The path swings left and heads west along the top of a cliff. The path eventually brings you to the *belvédère*, with some picnic tables close by (12).

The splendid view from the *belvédère*, on top of a cliff directly overlooking Nébias, is to be savoured. **Puivert castle** is prominent on the left; beyond that is the Lac de Montbel; far beyond is the Montagne Noire. The hills surrounding the Aude valley extend to the right. The flat area (former lake) is also directly below. Behind, to the south, are the bulky mountains in the direction of Usson.

On leaving the *belvédère*, continue west along the waymarked path. After a short distance it descends a

The imposing entrance to Puivert castle

little to come out of the woodland onto open ground. It meets a track where you turn right, to continue in what is still a westward direction. The track re-enters woodland and starts to go downhill. The slope becomes steeper and the track narrows to a path. After descending for some distance, be careful to take a waymarked left turn (13) down an even steeper path in the forest.

The path soon crosses a streambed. It becomes a track once again and starts to climb for a considerable distance through the forest. It bends to the left and terraces around the side of the hill.

Where your track is eventually joined by another forest track, coming up on the right, turn sharp right (14) and go down that other track. As you descend, you may see below on the left the upper end of a small lake – Lac de Tury. Watch out for and take a waymarked path which turns left off the track and descends to the shore of the lake. Cross the dam to meet the GR7 (15) on the other side. Turn right there.

Follow the GR7 along a stony track as it winds down through the forest. Not long after leaving the lake, you see some impressive limestone crags on the right. Your route then swings sharp right, and descends to cross a stream, where it turns to the left.

You soon come down to a more substantial forest track (16). Turn sharp left onto that track, then almost immediately turn right off it to descend into the forest once again. The GR7 now approximately follows the line of a rough forest track going down through the forest. But the actual waymarked route goes to the left and to the right of the track on the way down, perhaps to avoid the steepest sections, which may also be very muddy in wet weather.

Eventually leave the forest (17) and follow a lane straight ahead across open, almost level country. Nébias stands on a slope on the other side. In due course, and after the lane has swung to the left, come to a track crossing where you meet the Sentier Cathare again (8). Go straight across and follow your outward route back into Nébias (1).

POINTS OF INTEREST

Puivert castle and village: See Cathar history above. The castle is particularly well known for its sculptures of musicians with their instruments, a reminder of the castle's pre-crusade fame as a centre for music and culture. Re-created medieval instruments can be seen in the Salle de Musiciens. The castle, situated on a ridge with Puivert village wedged into a gap below, is open all year. The renowned museum in the village (the Musée du Quercorb), open from April to early November, has displays on local history and medieval musical instruments.

Nébias: This village has a small wildlife museum, open in July and August. The remains of a stone-built windmill sit on a hill to the north (passed on the northern walk), with a good view of Puivert castle to the west.

The **limestone plateau** immediately to the north of Nébias has been eroded in a most entertaining way. The rock has been carved into deep channels and depressions, linked up in an intricate fashion. Most of this karst landscape is also in a forest, which makes it doubly mystifying when you are trying to find your way through it.

Former lake: The large expanse of almost flat land stretching to the south of Nébias and Puivert was formerly occupied by a lake, covering nearly 200ha and about 15m deep. In the late 13th century the barrier at Puivert burst and the lake drained away, causing enormous damage in the valley downriver. Mirepoix was completely destroyed. (The current town of Mirepoix – a jewel of medieval architecture – was rebuilt on a different site.) Whether the catastrophe was the result of natural causes, or whether the lake was deliberately released – perhaps so that the land could be used for agriculture – remains unclear.

Visiting times

The walking time given for the northern walk doesn't allow time for playing around in the labyrinth. Even if you don't get lost, you can happily add another 1hr or so to your walk for weaving around the moss-covered rocks there.

Puivert castle and village: allow at least 1hr to visit the castle, and another hour or two to look around the museum in Puivert and the village.

Nébias museum: allow about 30min.

Further information

- These two circular walks are both described in a *Topo-guide* entitled *Aude en Pyrénées* (nos 3 and 4). Available, price 4 Euros, from Quillan tourist office: Maison du Tourisme 'Aude en Pyrénées', Square André Tricoire BP 8, 11500 Quillan; tel: (00 33) (0)4 68 20 07 78; tourisme.quillan@wanadoo.fr; **www.ville-quillan.fr**.

- The 'labyrinth' walk is also described in *Les Sentiers d'Emilie en Pays cathare* and the FFRP's *Topo-guide, L'Aude, Pays Cathare à pied* (see Appendix 2).
- For Puivert castle, museum and the surrounding area refer in particular to: Château de Puivert, 11230 Puivert; tel: (00 33) (0)4 68 20 81 52; infos@chateau-de-puivert.com; **www.chateau-de-puivert.com**.
- Musée du Quercorb, 16, rue Barry du Lion, 11230 Puivert; tel: (00 33) (0)04 68 20 80 98.
- Communauté de Communes du Chalabrais, Cours Sully, 11230 Chalabre; tel: (00 33) (0)4 68 69 21 94; chalabrais.ccc@free.fr; **www.quercorb.com**.

9 MONTSÉGUR

Montségur castle, located high on its steep-sided *pog*, is today the most powerful and probably best known of all the images associated with the Cathars and Cathar castle country. If you approach Montségur by road from the east, the *pog* looks not unlike a huge forearm and clenched fist, raised vertically towards the sky. Some might see that as a symbol of the Cathars' defiance in the face of certain defeat.

The pre-eminence of Montségur is celebrated with two first-class walks. Both are quite testing, but a shorter variant of one is also offered.

The Montségur castle walk is a circular route with stunning views of the castle, starting and finishing in Montferrier (1). It follows the Sentier Cathare up to Montségur castle, before a climb to nearly 1700m with close views of the superb mountains of the St-Barthélemy range. Finally, there is a descent to Montferrier via a woodland valley. A variant of this walk goes from Montferrier up to Montségur castle and back.

The Montségur mountain walk is a hard but immensely rewarding ascent of the Pic de St-Barthélemy (2348m), the highest point on all the walks in this book. The summit is approached from the north, starting near the Lac de Moulzoune (10). It follows a popular waymarked route which, on the ascent, passes two outstandingly wild and beautiful mountain lakes. A marvellous open ridge is followed in descent.

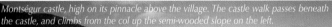

Montségur castle, high on its pinnacle above the village. The castle walk passes beneath the castle, and climbs from the col up the semi-wooded slope on the left.

CATHAR HISTORY: 1243–1244

Retaliation by the French and the Catholic Church for the Avignonet massacre came quickly. A decision was taken to destroy Montségur.

Raymond de Péreille (see Roquefixade, section 5) had rebuilt Montségur castle in 1204. It was well fortified, and became the Cathars' principal stronghold. The leaders of its church and many dispossessed Languedoc barons had all taken refuge there. The Cathar community at Montségur could count on strong moral and material support from the inhabitants of the surrounding villages.

Only a massive, sustained military assault on Montségur could breach its defences and wipe out the Cathar forces. The French left little to chance. They assembled an army of sufficient strength and sent it to besiege Montségur in the summer of 1243 – it must have numbered thousands. The defenders of Montségur totalled about 400, women and children included.

For all their huge superiority in arms and numbers, it took the French until March 1244 to subdue Montségur. To reach the castle walls they had to fight their way inch by inch up a steep slope on the east side of the *pog*. When the Cathars realised that further resistance was futile, they negotiated a two-week truce and prepared for their fate.

On 16 March the defenders of Montségur marched out of the castle and down to the foot of the *pog*. Those who would not renounce their faith were thrown – or threw themselves – onto a huge bonfire. Over 200 Cathars died in that way. Those who escaped or otherwise survived knew that Montségur would never again be a Cathar sanctuary.

Later events

The castle was destroyed. The French built a new fortress on the site later in the 13th century, serving a purely military purpose. When the border between France and Spain moved south in 1659, the castle was abandoned.

PRACTICAL INFORMATION
Access to starting points

By road from Lavelanet, take the D117 in the direction of Foix and turn left just after leaving Lavelanet to go through Villeneuve d'Olmes along the D9 to Montferrier. Keep to the D9 as it passes to the south of Montferrier. Just after passing Montferrier's museum, on the right, there is a bridge over the river on the right. The castle walk starts by that bridge.

For the mountain walk, continue along the D9 in the direction of Montségur and soon turn right onto the D909, which leads to the ski resort of les Monts d'Olmes. After some zigzags and bends, the road curves to the left, after which turn sharp left onto a forest track heading for Moulzoune. In an open area in a valley reached after about 3km, there is a car park on the right; the walk starts there.

Public transport in this area is scarce.

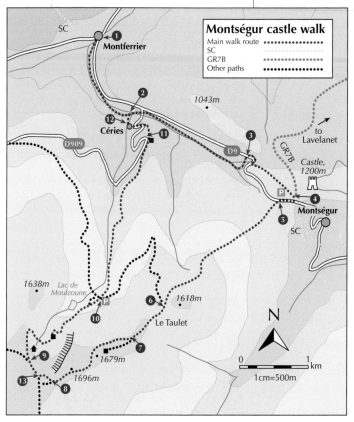

121

Navigation

Castle walk: from Montferrier (1) to Montségur (4) the walk follows the Sentier Cathare (red and yellow waymarking). The rest of the walk – until it rejoins the Sentier Cathare at point (2) just above Montferrier – carries yellow waymarks. From point (2) retrace your steps back to the start, along the Sentier Cathare.

Mountain walk: most of the walk is indicated by yellow waymarks. However, from points (15) to (17) – just above the Étang des Truites to the summit – waymarks are yellow and red. That section is on a regional long-distance path, the Tour du Massif de Tabe.

There are helpful path signposts at various points along the mountain walk and on the higher sections of the castle walk. But please note that several of those signposts were in a damaged state when the walks were surveyed for this book. The painted waymarks on rocks, trees, etc were reasonably clear.

Bear in mind that the mountain walk in particular has sections along scree, rocky slopes and boulder fields. Across such sections in particular the line of the path is not always clear and the waymarks may be tricky to spot in mist. Make sure that you can navigate with map and compass over such terrain before attempting this walk.

Note too that between Lac de Moulzoune (10) and Le Taulet (6) there are also other path waymarks (green). These can be ignored.

ROUTE DESCRIPTION – MONTSÉGUR CASTLE WALK AND VARIANT

Distances:	main walk 14km (8.7 miles); variant 9km (5.6 miles)
Time:	main walk 6hr; variant 3hr
Altitude:	690m to 1650m
Maps:	IGN 1:25,000 2147ET (Foix Tarascon-sur-Ariège) and 2247OT (Lavelanet); Montségur castle is in map fold 2C of the Lavelanet map

This walk starts where the Sentier Cathare heads south out of **Montferrier** (1), by the bridge over the wide Touyre river. Facing south, a campsite lies straight ahead and the central part of the village can be seen on the other side of the river. Follow the tarmacked lane which goes to the right of the campsite, with the river on your right. Yellow and red waymarks indicate that you are on the Sentier Cathare.

Looking back to Montségur castle from the long climb up to Le Taulet on the castle walk

After a short distance the lane bears left and climbs a little. At two successive crossings with other tarmacked lanes, go straight across, up the valley. Running close to a stream on the left, your route then passes through the outskirts of Montferrier. It soon becomes a footpath and enters more open country.

You eventually come to a path junction (2). Your route lies to the left, along the Sentier Cathare. ▶

The Sentier Cathare goes along the edge of a large meadow, which rises up the slope on your right. It bears to the left and fords the stream you have been following. In the meadow on the other side, it continues parallel to the stream, with the D909 close by on the left. You soon reach and cross the D909, continuing on the waymarked path straight ahead. Enter woodland and climb steadily; sections of the path can be quite wet and muddy, even in periods of dry weather. The route is obvious and there are hardly any other paths in the valley.

Follow the path up to near the head of the valley. There it meets a track; turn sharp left onto that track.

Emerge from the woodland and reach a gate by the D9 (3). Go through the gate, turn right, and follow the

At (2) the path on the right – sign-posted for Céries – is the return route.

road verge. In clear weather ahead is a stunning view of **Montségur castle** perched high on its immense isolated rock pinnacle. The outer foothills of the Pyrenees stretch out to the north. Beyond is an area of lowland, and beyond that the huge upturned hull of land which is the western end of the Montagne Noire.

Follow the road as it turns sharp right then, by a small brown cliff, turn sharp left up a track which almost immediately enters woodland. The path climbs steeply through the woods. Eventually the slope levels out, and soon afterwards Montségur castle becomes visible again on the left.

Reach an intersection of paths (4) with the GR7B coming up on the left and, crossing the Sentier Cathare, the path which links a roadside car park on the right to the castle high up on the left. (Come back to this crossing if you now walk up to visit the castle.)

Turn right and almost immediately come down to the D9. Turn right and walk up that road for a little way, almost to the brow of the hill. Turn left there (5) and, with Montségur castle directly behind you, follow a slightly sunken grass lane which climbs straight up the shoulder of the open hillside ahead.

You now have 1hr or more of steady, hard climbing. The route carries yellow waymarks and is pretty obvious for most of the way. The first part, in open country, generally follows the line of the sunken lane. Sections may be overgrown and you will need to walk alongside the lane in the adjoining meadows. Before you enter the woodland higher up, be sure to look back to enjoy the stupendous views towards Montségur castle. **Montségur village** is down on the right. The crag on which sits Roquefixade castle, in the distance on the left, may also be visible. In the lower country to the north, beyond Montségur, is the sizeable town of Lavelanet and the Lac de Montbel.

Shortly after passing a ruined stone cabin, on your left, fork right, as indicated by the waymarks. Enter woodland and the climb becomes notably steeper. On entering a patch of open ground, the path swings to the left a little, then bears to the right and re-enters woodland. Not long after you emerge into open ground above tree level, the slope of the path eases considerably. Eventually, you cross a fence and come to a signposted path intersection (6).

The castle walk continues straight ahead. You are now on a broad ridge of upland grazing land, Le Taulet. Cross to the left-hand side of the ridgeline and come to a path fork (7). The waymarks tell you to go left, but it is probably better to fork right. Pass below and to the right of both a shepherd's cabin and a rock pinnacle, rising to 1679m.

On reaching a grassy col, the path swings to the left a little and passes below and to the left of a hill rising to 1696m. The high mountains lie directly ahead and in clear weather the view from here towards those is magnificent.

The path becomes a terrace in the hillside and you enter an area of irregular ground marked by former quarrying. As you approach a rocky col on the right, avoid the temptation to contour round to that col and instead follow a stony waymarked path descending to the left.

At the bottom of a gully, with the col above on your right, follow the waymarked path up the slope directly ahead. Keep clear of the boulder scree over on the right, which may be unstable and dangerous. Reach a track on a hillside terrace. Straight ahead are ruined buildings associated with the former quarry here. Turn right, along the track (8). ▶

From (8), a waymarked path climbs a slope to the left and heads up towards the Pic de St-Barthélemy.

Pass to the left of the col and you will see, on the right, the top of a huge quarry on the other side of the ridge that you have just walked along.

The track weaves around and reaches a signposted path intersection (13). ▶

From (13) the path going uphill, sharp left leads to the Pic St-Barthélemy, on the mountain walk described below.

The castle walk continues straight ahead. After a short distance come to a path fork (9), where you go right. You very soon start to descend along a grass track into the Moulzoune valley, on your right. Pass, on your right, a stone cabin (part of which offers shelter to walkers).

The track swings sharp right and descends towards the woodland below. Pass, on your left, a large, ruined

The Pic de St-Barthélemy, as seen from near Montségur

stone building. Directly in front is a huge quarried rock face. The route now turns sharp left down what is signposted as a path diversion. Follow a wide, relatively new forest road which zigzags down through the beech wood into the valley. At a gate you meet, on the right, the former route, which appears to have become blocked by a rockfall.

You soon pass, on your left, the Lac de Moulzoune, a pretty picnic spot. A notice indicates that the lake is being used for the restocking of Atlantic salmon. The route continues down a track on the right. A little further along, where the waymarks follow the track to the left, you can cut off a bend in the track by going straight down through the beech woodland towards the car park below (10). ◀

The car park (10) is the starting point for the mountain walk, below.

Go straight across the forest road just below the car park. The shady track beyond is very pleasant and easy to follow. It goes down the axis of the valley, with a stream on the left. After some distance, you can see the D909 below. Go left at a couple of track forks and soon

126

afterwards reach a patch of open ground with a house on the right. Go left and immediately meet the D909 at a sharp bend in that road (11).

The next section of the path is not well waymarked and at first may be overgrown. Without going along the road at all, the route goes straight down the steep, semi-wooded slope ahead, to cut off a large bend in the road. In practice you may have to walk along the road to the left for a few metres, step over the metal crash barrier, scramble down a grass embankment, then continue down the steep slope ahead. You will see yellow waymarks further down the slope.

Reach another hairpin bend in the D909. Turn left and walk down the road to the hamlet of Céries (12). Leave the D909, cross a bridge at the entrance to the hamlet, then immediately turn right to follow a track going downhill with a stream on the right. The track becomes a path. It may be a little overgrown, but you soon meet the Sentier Cathare (2), where you turn left. Follow that trail back into Montferrier (1).

Variant
Follow the route of the castle walk, starting from Montferrier (1) and climbing to the foot of the hill on which Montségur castle is located (4). Return by the same route.

ROUTE DESCRIPTION – MONTSÉGUR MOUNTAIN WALK

Distance:	14km (8.7 miles)
Time:	7hr
Altitude:	1300m to 2348m
Map:	IGN 1:25,000 2147ET (Foix Tarascon-sur-Ariège); the whole of the mountain walk is on this map; Lac de Moulzoune is in map fold 4G

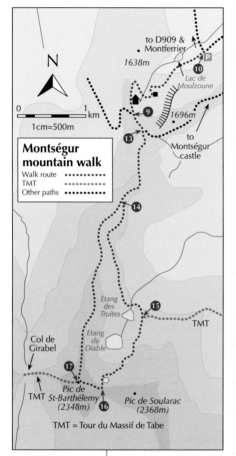

This walk begins at the car park (10) on a forest road just below and to the north of Lac de Moulzoune.

Take a track, indicated by yellow waymarks, heading up into the forest above the car park. It winds up the valley and soon emerges into an open space by Lac de Moulzoune (on your right).

Follow the track up into the forest to the left of the lake. You come to a gate where the former route went straight on, towards a huge quarry face. The route has now been diverted to the right, up a steep, wide and relatively new forest road, which zigzags up through beech woodland.

Emerge into another open space with, on your right, a large, ruined stone building. The track swings to the right, crosses the head of a stream and climbs above the tree line. It then turns sharp left, passes to the right of a stone cabin and soon arrives on the spur of a hill at the head of the valley.

At a path junction (9), meet another waymarked trail coming up from a valley on your right. Carry straight on. You very soon come to a path fork (13), where you climb the slope to the right. ◀

The path on the left at (13), which approaches old quarry workings, is followed on the castle walk, above.

Reach the long ridge heading roughly north from the Pic de St-Barthélemy. Turn right and follow the path

128

passing just to the right of the ridgeline. This well-used path soon meets the ridgeline again, and shortly curves around the hillside to the left of and below that ridgeline.

After meeting the ridgeline again at a minor col, the path once again swings left. It curves around the hillside to the left of and below the ridgeline. Watch carefully for a path fork. This fork is waymarked but, at the time this walk was surveyed, a signpost at this point had been

Etang des Truites (Trout Lake), on the mountain walk to the Pic de St-Barthélemy

129

removed. At the path fork (14), go left and start to descend the hillside on the left.

The path then bears to the right, contouring around the head of a valley basin. Beyond that, it goes to the left of a large boulder field, twisting between rocks through an area of rhododendrons and pine trees. The path then climbs and descends in this fashion for some distance, with the main ridge above to the right and the mountain peaks straight ahead.

Eventually, reach the exquisitely beautiful Étang des Truites (a mountain lake which is indeed fished for trout). From here the path immediately ahead is not entirely clear, but the best route is probably as follows. Cross the stream near the lip of the lake and head back, away from the lake for a short distance. Then turn hard right and climb a ridge which enters pine forest and passes to the left of and above the lake. In due course, you meet, slightly on the left, a regional long-distance path – the Tour du Massif de Tabe. At the path junction (15), turn right and follow what are now red and yellow waymarks. The Pic de Soularac looms immediately above the path here, but the steep climb ahead is making for the Pic de St-Barthélemy, over to your right.

Pass high above the Étang du Diable, on your right – another wonderful sight. Swing a little to the left, then scramble up a particularly steep section of the route on the right. This brings you to an area of relatively level ground with a couple of small lakes. This lies just below a col between the summits of Soularac, to the left, and St-Barthélemy, to the right. Walk up to the col (16). The Ariège valley suddenly comes into view and the Ariège–Andorra mountains stretch across the distant horizon. Turn right here and scramble up the summit ridge to the Pic de St-Barthélemy (17).

The view from the summit on a fine day is vast and mesmerising. Immediately to the east is the rocky eagle's nest of the Pic de Soularac, at 2368m the highest point in Cathar castle country. To the south and west stretch range upon range of Pyrenees mountains. To the north the distant Lac de Montbel is a clear landmark, with

Montségur castle also visible; the Pech de Bugarach stands out prominently on the right. From here you can see the greater part of the country traversed by the Sentier Cathare, from the outskirts of Foix to the Corbières hills. ▶

For the return journey, follow the ridge heading north, away from the summit. The route is occasionally marked by yellow waymarks, but don't rely on them. At first, the ridge is covered with immense boulders. Pick your way carefully across those. Your descent along this section is also pretty steep and continues to be so for some way. Eventually, the slope becomes

In mist, be careful not to descend from the summit of the Pic de St-Barthélemy to the west, to the Col de Girabel, indicated by red and yellow waymarks.

Walkers descending from the Pic de St-Barthélemy on a ridge followed on the mountain walk

more moderate and boulders and scree give way to high mountain pasture.

Where the path curves around the hillside to the right of and below the ridgeline, come to the path fork (14) from where, on your outward journey, you turned away from the ridge to head for the Étang des Truites.

Retrace your steps from here. Follow the path ahead as it descends roughly along the line of the ridge. As you approach the old quarry workings, be careful to bear left, towards the hill spur at the head of the Moulzoune valley.

On that spur, you meet the path followed by the castle walk on the right (13). A short distance further along, fork right (9) and descend into the Moulzoune valley. Take care to stay on the outward route and in due course you will be back at the start (10).

POINTS OF INTEREST

Montferrier: This attractive little town has a museum of local life, industries and history, open from June to November.

Montségur castle: Most Cathar castles probably bear little or no resemblance to how they appeared in the Cathar period, and Montségur is a good example. It is also a memorable (and moving) experience to scale the hill which the Cathars defended so tenaciously in the winter of 1243–44, and to look down from the castle walls as members of that besieged community did, knowing that they were staring at their place of execution.

The castle is open all year, except in January. There is a climb of about 170m from the foot of the hill to the castle.

Montségur village and museum: There is evidence of human settlement on the *pog* dating back to prehistoric times. After the siege ended in 1244, the Cathar settlement on the *pog* was destroyed, and a new village developed lower down (Montségur's present location).

There is very little motor traffic in the village, and it is a delight to stroll around. The museum is fascinating. It mostly contains relics of everyday life in the Cathar settlement on the *pog*, such as coins and domestic utensils. It also displays remnants of some of the weapons used in the fighting during the siege, for example sword blades, and the heavy stone balls that were hurled by a giant catapult against the castle walls. The museum is open all year, except in January.

Visiting times
Allow at least 1.5hr for the climb to, visit of and descent from Montségur castle, starting at the foot of the hill. It would be feasible to combine a visit to the castle with the variant, and it might just be possible to combine the castle visit with the main castle walk. If you tackle the mountain walk, save your castle visit for another day.

Allow about 1hr each for the museums in Montségur and Montferrier.

Further information

- The castle walk follows part of the Sentier Cathare and also part of no 14 in *Topo-guide, Pays d'Olmes*, published by the Communauté de Communes Pays d'Olmes (see below), price 2 Euros (2004). The mountain walk is no 16. Communauté de Communes Pays d'Olmes: 32 rue Jean Jaurès, 09300 Lavelanet; tel: (00 33) (0)5 34 09 33 80; tourisme@paysdolmes.org; **www.paysdolmes.org**.

- Lavelanet tourist office (where the *Topo-guide, Pays d'Olmes* can be bought): Maison de Lavelanet, BP 89–09300 Lavelanet; tel: (00 33) (0)5 61 01 22 20; lavelanet.tourisme@wanadoo.fr.

- Local sources of information on Montségur castle and museum are Office du tourisme, 09300 Montségur; tel: (00 33) (0)5 61 03 03 03; info.tourisme@montsegur.org; **www.montsegur.org**.

- Montségur mairie: (00 33) (0)5 61 01 10 27; mairie.montsegur@wanadoo.fr; **www.citaenet.com/montsegur**.

- Montferrier museum: (00 33) (0)5 61 01 91 47.

10 USSON

This walk is an all-day figure-of-eight circuit, starting in the village of le Puch, in the centre. The northern loop passes close to Usson castle and the southern loop goes beneath Quérigut castle. Either loop can be used as a shorter, half-day walk in its own right.

The walk climbs and descends all the time, but is no more than moderately strenuous. It follows waymarked paths and tracks through flower-rich meadows and forests over the hills of the Pays de Donézan. This is an upland valley basin in Ariège, bounded to the east by the deep Aude valley and on all other sides by mountains and hills. The landscape is dotted with granite tors; many of the buildings in Donézan's villages are built of granite.

CATHAR HISTORY: 1244

Standing high on a spur in the upper Aude valley, Usson castle was another mountain stronghold of the Cathars. During the siege of Montségur, the leading Cathars feared the worst and decided to put at least their money out of reach of their French oppressors. In December 1243 two Cathars managed to slip out of the castle and pass through the French defences. They carried with them a quantity of gold and silver – the famous 'treasure' of the Cathar church. They hid it in a cave somewhere in the region.

One of the two men returned to Montségur in February 1244. He no doubt explained where the treasure had been hidden. On the night before Montségur was surrendered, in March, four Bons Hommes stole away from the castle by descending a cliff below the fortress. They carried nothing with them, but the assumption is that their mission was to recover the treasure.

Some time later two of the four reached a surviving Cathar community in Italy. One supposition is that they brought the treasure with them. There are many other theories about the its fate; whatever the truth, it seems that, en route for Italy, the four *Bons Hommes* stopped at the castle of Usson.

The owners of Usson castle paid for their resistance to the French; one of them, Bernard d'Alion, was burnt at the stake by the Inquisition in 1258.

Quérigut castle, a few kilometres to the south of Usson, and passed on this walk, also gave refuge to Cathars.

Later events

Usson castle served as a frontier fortress during subsequent centuries. In the 18th century it was rebuilt and became the home of a local aristocrat. The castle was sold after the Revolution, used as a quarry for its stone, and fell into ruin. In the past few years substantial restoration work has begun.

Quérigut castle also served as a frontier fortress after the Cathar period. It too fell into ruin and was heavily pillaged. Little of the castle remains today, but its surviving walls still present an impressive sight.

PRACTICAL INFORMATION

Access to starting point

By road from Quillan, go south on the D117, signposted for Perpignan. After passing through the narrow Pierre-Lys gorge, turn right onto the D118, signposted for Axat and Font-Romeu. Just after Usson-les-Bains, turn right onto the D16. That road soon passes below Usson castle, with a car park for visitors on the left. For le Puch, continue on the D16 through Rouze then, at le Pla, turn left onto the D25, which climbs to le Puch.

Usson castle

Public transport in this area is scarce.

Navigation

Some sections of the walk follow local walking circuits and carry yellow waymarks – (1) to (6) on the northern loop, and (1) to (12) on the southern loop. Other sections follow the Tour du Donézan, with red and yellow waymarks – (6) to (1) on the northern loop, and (12) to (1) on the southern loop. Other waymarked routes branch off from and meet the route described, so take care not to wander off along one of those.

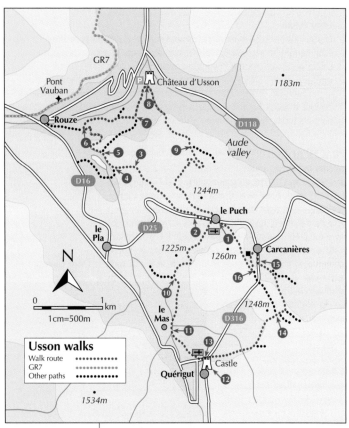

GR7

Pont Vauban

Château d'Usson

1183m

Rouze

D118

Aude valley

8

7

6

5   3

9

4

D16

1244m

le Puch

2   1   Carcanières

le Pla

1225m   1260m   15

N

16

0   1 km

1cm=500m

10   1248m

D316

le Mas

11

13

12

14

Usson walks
Walk route   ●●●●●●●●●
GR7   ●●●●●●●●●
Other paths   ●●●●●●●●●

Castle

Quérigut

1534m

ROUTE DESCRIPTION

The starting point is on the D25 at the eastern entrance to le Puch village (1).

A road forks to your left to go past the village church. Leave that and fork right to follow the D25 through le Puch village. Go straight on where red and yellow waymarks indicate a turning to the right (the return route at the end of the northern loop). You will soon start to see yellow waymarks along the way.

Distance:	16km (9.9 miles)
Time:	5.5hr (northern loop, passing Usson castle, 3hr; southern loop, passing Quérigut castle, 2.5hr)
Altitude:	900m to 1220m
Map:	IGN 1:25,000 2248ET (Axat Quérigut); Usson castle is in map fold 5C

Not long after the road leaves the village, take a grass track forking off to the right (2), signposted for Rouze. Follow this path for some distance; it shows signs of being quite an old route between villages in Donézan. It descends gradually alongside meadows and patches of woodland, with fine views to le Pla below, and to the high hills and mountain forests beyond.

Eventually, your path bears to the left (3) and goes straight down the hillside. In the valley below is a small lake with a power station at its northern end. Towards the bottom of the slope, as the track you are on swings to the left; be careful to follow the waymarked route as it turns to the right (4) and traverses the hillside.

A little further on the path swings sharply to the left and reaches a narrow tarmacked lane. Turn sharp right and follow that lane for a short distance. Where the lane begins to bend round to the right, by some poplar trees, fork off to the left, onto a grass track (5). This climbs gently.

Rouze village lies below. Above and beyond Rouze can be seen the track which is today followed by the GR7 long-distance path. It traverses the lower part of the slope above Rouze. It marks the route of the Chemin des Canons. The restored **Pont Vauban** along that track may also be visible from here.

Your track soon swings to the right and enters an area of woodland. The path starts to zigzag down the slope on the left, staying in woodland nearly all the while. As you descend you may catch a glimpse of the remains of **Usson castle**, on a hill about 1km away.

Eventually the path comes down to a point where there is a bridge on the left crossing a fast-flowing mountain stream (6), issuing from the lake seen earlier.

The track which goes over the bridge heads for the village of Rouze, not far away. You may like to visit Rouze, especially if you are only walking the northern loop. The Tour de France came through the village in 2003. There, the cyclists steeled themselves for the stiff climb up to the col de Pailhères, west of Rouze. Although over 2000m in altitude, the road over that col is the only one directly linking Donézan to the rest of Ariège. If you visit Rouze, retrace your steps to the bridge where you left the main route.

Leave the bridge on your left and take the track going off to the right through the woods. The stream falls away rapidly on your left. Your path is now indicated by red and yellow waymarks; follow these all the way back to le Puch.

Where a path goes down on the left, keep to the track which forks to the right. In due course you meet – near more open country – a steep, stony track coming down on your right. Turn left there (7). Not long afterwards you leave the woodland entirely. Meet an access road coming up from the valley on your left, and suddenly directly ahead lie the impressive remains of Usson castle (8).

The walk continues along a grass track, which turns sharp right off the access road near the entrance to the castle. The track zigzags up the hillside, passing a covered reservoir on the left. It then makes a long, winding ascent up the shoulder of the hill ahead. It crosses semi-open country abounding in wild flowers, with occasional views back down to Usson castle. The panorama over the Aude valley (a long way down on your left) and across to the hills and mountains encircling Donézan becomes more impressive the higher you climb.

Eventually the path comes to a gate (9) with, straight ahead, a forest track. Go through the gate, then follow the track to the right as it climbs into a forest. The long ascent continues, with the track in due course winding around to the right and emerging into more open country.

The slope now eases off and, as the track bears round to the left, it becomes a magnificent balcony path. You have the best views so far of much of Donézan and of the mountains around this extremely pretty region.

Finally, the track approaches and enters le Puch village. Carry straight on through the village until you descend to meet the D25. Turn left there and soon return to the start of this northern loop (1). ▶

The southern loop begins by following the lower road through le Puch as it passes to the left of a church. Just beyond the village, you should see a footpath

To continue the walk and complete the southern loop, turn sharp right at (1).

Fountain in the centre of Quérigut village

signpost indicating that Quérigut is 1hr away. The road swings around to the left and approaches a cemetery. Turn right and pass below the cemetery. From here your route to Quérigut is indicated by yellow waymarks.

The unsurfaced lane which you are now on is bounded by granite boulder walls and winds through very pleasant, semi-wooded country. Granite tors and boulders are a distinct feature of the landscape. Eventually the path swings sharply to the right, and descends. **Quérigut castle** and village come into view. On meeting another waymarked path on the right (10), bear left, following the direction indicated by a signpost for Quérigut.

The path terraces across the hillside and approaches a mountain stream on the right. The route appears to swing to the right over a bridge which crosses that stream, but you must take a less well-defined path which goes up on the left *without* crossing the stream (11).

This path climbs steeply for quite some distance. Higher up, where the slope eases off, it becomes a farm track. That track emerges onto a motor road just below a cemetery. With the cemetery on your left, follow the road up towards Quérigut village, which is now close by. However, note a road turning on the left where the D316 heads off towards Carcanières. You should return to this point shortly, but meanwhile you can go straight up into Quérigut to explore the castle remains (a short distance up on the left [12]), and the village itself.

Returning to the bottom of the village, just above the cemetery, follow the D316 on the right signposted for Carcanières. Where – just after leaving the village behind – the road bears to the left, take a track which forks off to the right (13). This track contours across the hillside. It carries red and yellow waymarks, and these indicate your route all the way from here to le Puch. Looking back, you should see Quérigut castle rising high above the village.

Where the track forks, bear left. Pass through a couple of cattle gates and continue straight ahead, as the track goes uphill. On approaching a small col at the top of the slope, go straight ahead where another track goes off to the left (14), then fork left. As you go down on the other side, you will see another track just below. Turn sharp left onto that track. You should soon see reassuring red and yellow waymarks on the track ahead. On either side are patches of mixed woodland, vegetable plots, stone walls, rocky hillsides and wild-flower-rich meadows.

The route rolls across the hillside, and is met by another track coming up on the right. You then see Carcanières village ahead. Where you meet again the D316 (15), there is, on the right, a map of all the walking routes in Donézan.

Go straight ahead along the D316 through the village, forking to the left and passing to the right of a

Access to the scant, but imposing, remains of Quérigut castle is via a stone staircase from the village war memorial

141

church. On coming down to a T-junction with the D25, turn left. After climbing for a short distance, turn sharp left onto a tarmacked lane. The lane doubles back, above the village.

After climbing for a little way, meet another lane on the right. Turn sharp right onto that lane (16). The lane approaches a farmstead. Just before the entrance, turn left onto a grass path. That path swings left around a granite outcrop, after which le Puch village comes into view below on the left.

The path descends to meet the D25. The start of the walk is a few metres down that road on the left (1).

POINTS OF INTEREST

Pont Vauban: This restored stone bridge near Rouze lies on an old road (the Chemin des Canons) constructed over 300 years ago to bring cannon and reinforcements to Mont Louis, further to the south.

Usson castle: The entrance to the castle is via an adjacent *Maison du Patrimoine* (visitor centre and museum of archaeology and local history). The castle remains tower above the deep Aude valley. The castle and *Maison de Patrimoine* are open every day in July and August; during the rest of the year they are mostly open only at weekends during the afternoon.

Quérigut castle: The remains of this fortress loom over the village, seeming to grow out of the huge boss of granite on which they are perched. The castle seems permanently open, with steps leading up to it from a war memorial opposite a school. There is no charge for entry.

Visiting times
Allow about 1.5hr for a visit to Usson castle and its exhibition. Allow about 30min for a visit to Quérigut castle.

Further information
- This walk links sections of waymarked circuits described in a collection published in 1998 by the Donézan Office de Tourisme, titled *Pays de Donézan*; price 10 Euros.
- Office de Tourisme du Donézan, 09460 le Pla; tel: (00 33) (0) 4 68 20 41 37; ot@donezan.com; **www.donezan.com**.
- Usson castle *Maison du Patrimoine*: (00 33) (0) 4 68 20 43 92.

11 PUILAURENS

This is a circular walk of moderate length, which winds up and down through a forest on a steep hillside. The forest is managed for timber production, but has a wide range of species and many impressive specimens. From time to time there are stunning views over the limestone peaks and deep valleys in this part of Cathar castle country. On the early and later sections of the walk there are striking views of Puilaurens castle.

The walk starts and finishes by the ticket office, just below Puilaurens castle. A walker's link to that office, from the nearest point accessible by public transport (the village of Lapradelle), is also described.

CATHAR HISTORY: 1244–1250

Puilaurens castle, located on a high, rocky pinnacle in a huge forest south of Quillan, is an extremely imposing medieval fortress. However, its vast, formidable appearance is almost entirely the result of reconstruction work carried out after the Cathars had been suppressed in the region.

Despite their dominance in the plains, the French forces could not easily control settlements and fortresses in the mountainous parts of the Cathars' domain. In such areas the Cathar faith still enjoyed firm support among wealthy and poor alike. So it was to places of security in such regions – notably Puilaurens – that the remaining *Bons Hommes* and *Bonnes Dames* retreated after the fall of Montségur. The *Bonne Dame* Saurine Rigaud was given shelter there from 1246–47.

Puilaurens castle was taken over by the French king around 1250, after which time it must be assumed that the fortress no longer served as a Cathar refuge.

Later events
In 1255 the French king ordered that Puilaurens be fortified as a frontier citadel. It became the strongest French bastion facing Spain until the Treaty of the Pyrenees in 1659. After that, the familiar story was repeated – abandonment, deterioration, and finally, in our own time, restoration of the castle's remains.

Puilaurens castle stands high above the village of Lapradelle

Note: Do not confuse Puilaurens – also spelt Puylaurens – in the *département* of Aude, with Puylaurens – in the *département* of Tarn – about 45km east of Toulouse (where there was also support for Cathars).

PRACTICAL INFORMATION
Access to starting points

There is a regular – though not very frequent – bus service to Lapradelle from Quillan and Perpignan. The summer tourist train between Rivesaltes (near Perpignan) and Axat also stops at Lapradelle. By road from Quillan, go south on the D117 (the main road to Perpignan) until you reach Lapradelle.

To proceed by motor vehicle from Lapradelle to Puilaurens castle, turn right there onto the D22. Shortly after passing through Puilaurens village, turn right onto the signposted access road climbing towards Puilaurens castle. That road ends in a car park by both a picnic area and the ticket office, which serves as the entrance to the castle.

Navigation

The walk from the ticket office below Puilaurens castle follows a wide forest track for almost its whole length. At first the route is indicated by the blue and yellow waymarks of the Sentier Cathare's southern 'variant', then – from point (8) back to the start – it is indicated by yellow waymarks.

The walker's link from Lapradelle at first follows the D22, before turning off onto a signposted path which climbs through the forest and carries yellow waymarks.

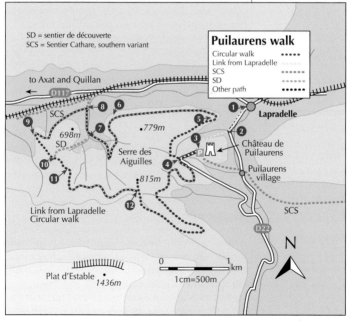

SD = sentier de découverte
SCS = Sentier Cathare, southern variant

Puilaurens walk

Circular walk	•••••
Link from Lapradelle	
SCS	•••••••
SD	
Other path	•••••

to Axat and Quillan

D117

SCS

⑨ 698m
SD

⑧ ⑥
⑦   •779m

⑩

⑪

Serre des Aiguilles

④

•815m

⑫

Link from Lapradelle
Circular walk

❶
Lapradelle

❷
Château de Puilaurens

❸ P 🏰

Puilaurens village

SCS

D22

N

Plat d'Estable
1436m

0   1 km
1cm=500m

145

ROUTE DESCRIPTION

Distances:	Lapradelle to castle ticket office 4km/2.5 miles (there and back); circular walk 12km (7.5 miles)
Times:	Lapradelle to castle ticket office 1hr (ascent), 45min (descent); circular walk 3.5hr
Altitude:	440m (Lapradelle) and 540m (ticket office) to 815m
Map:	IGN 1:25,000 2348ET (Prades St-Paul-de-Fenouillet) ; Puilaurens castle is in map fold 1B

Link from Lapradelle

From the centre of this village (1), by the bridge over the river coming down from the south (from Puilaurens) take the D22, signposted at its junction with the main D117 for the Château de Puilaurens. Walk along this road through the village. Just beyond the village, pass a large building on the left (shown on the map as a sawmill), then see on the right – opposite some conifers above the river on the left – the start of a path (2) with yellow waymarks. This path is clearly signposted for Puilaurens castle.

This well-used path is steep and rocky at first, then climbs steadily through the forest. It eventually brings you to a col (3) by a car park, picnic site and a ticket office for the castle. The castle is on the left, reached by following a wide path through the woods.

Circular walk

From the ticket office, go away from the castle, by following a wide tarmacked road ahead. This is the access road for motor vehicles to the castle. After a short distance, the access road bends to the left (4). There is an open area for parking on the right, and, beyond that, just on the edge of the forest, well-made jeep tracks go off right and left. Take the track on the right. It is signposted as the Sentier Cathare (the 'southern variant'). This section of the Sentier Cathare has waymarks with blue, yellow and orange stripes.

Almost the whole walk – which eventually returns to this point – follows this track. Except where otherwise directed below, keep to this track and ignore other, usually less well-made tracks leading from it into the forest.

The track contours round to the right. There are very fine views on your right towards **Puilaurens castle**, perched on a rocky, steep-sided, isolated hill. Behind, towering above the forest to the south and visible during much of this walk, are the immense limestone crags of the Plat d'Estable, rising to nearly 1500m. The track eventually turns sharp left (5). There follows a long, straight stretch of track, with the main east–west D117 far below, in a valley on the right. There is little waymarking on this stretch, but it is not really necessary.

Where the track eventually bends to the left (6), there is ahead the first of several fine views westwards up the deep, rugged, heavily wooded Rebenty valley. In the far distance you may be able to see mountains which rise to an altitude of about 2000m and which are not far from Montségur.

The track now swings fairly steeply downhill, twisting left and right as it does so. Towards the bottom of its descent, it turns right (7).

At (7) you will see on the left a big display panel and a signpost just below it saying '*Départ*'. This is the start of the *sentier de découverte* (an 'interpretation trail' in British jargon). It is quite a pleasant and interesting circuit, with with clear yellow waymarks. All the information panels along the way are in French, but if you can read a little you will learn a lot about the forest. If you follow this trail (at least 1hr), you descend eventually to this starting point, where you can rejoin the circular walk.

The main route itself descends northwards from point (7), with a fast-flowing stream on the right. It emerges on the edge of an open area (8) in the east–west

147

From the highest point on the Puilaurens walk, you look straight down upon the castle

From (8) the Sentier Cathare goes straight ahead, across the open area; shortly afterwards it turns left to head west towards Axat.

valley followed by the D117. Here you turn left, by a yellow waymark. ◀

Your track now starts to climb up through the forest. Look out for yellow waymarks for the rest of this walk. After winding uphill for some way, the track turns sharp left (9). Straight ahead – and then on your right as you follow the track round the spur of the hill – there are once again magnificent views up the Rebenty valley.

A little further on the track forks, and you go left. A little beyond that, the *sentier de découverte* comes up from the left to meet your track (10). A short distance beyond that – just before the track bends left to cross a small valley – a path leads up, right, into the forest to an information panel by an impressive fir tree. The panel describes this type of tree – *le sapin pectiné* – as 'the king of the forest' (the forests of the Pyrenees).

After another short distance along the main track, the *sentier de découverte* turns off left (11) to descend steeply to its starting point. The main track continues to wind steadily uphill, with the impressive slopes of the forest falling away on your left.

Eventually you reach a col (12), from where a sign-posted path goes steeply up on the left towards a prominent summit at 815m, the Serre des Aiguilles. Climb up that path. Just before you reach the very top, take a path going into the undergrowth on the right. After a few metres there is a stunning view of Puilaurens castle down below, with colossal limestone pyramids just beyond. Far over on the left can be seen the striking profile of the Pech de Bugarach. From the other side of the hill you are standing on, looking in the opposite direction, you have the finest of this walk's magnificent views to the west, up the Rebenty valley and beyond.

Go back to the col at the foot of the Serre des Aiguilles; turn left and continue to follow the wide forest track. After climbing a little, the track starts its long, gentle, winding descent back to Puilaurens castle. From several points you have superb views of the castle, as it becomes ever closer. You finally reach the tarmacked access road (4) leading to the castle. Follow that road back to the ticket office at the foot of the castle's hill (3). ▶

If returning on foot to Lapradelle from (3), retrace your steps back down the foot-path (signposted for Lapradelle) to the D22 road (2), then turn left along that road to reach Lapradelle village (1).

The impregnable outer wall of Puilaurens castle

149

POINTS OF INTEREST

Puilaurens castle: This is one of the best preserved of the 'Cathar castles', and has been described as 'a model of medieval military architecture'. The castle is open every day from April to October and during weekends in February, March and November. It is closed in December and January (except in the Christmas holiday period). The castle is about 150m above the ticket office.

Alongside the path which leads up to the castle from the ticket office are several planted **shrubs and trees** typical of this region. Signs indicate their names in French. They include: *alisier* (service tree – *Sorbus domestica*); *bruyère* (heather); *buis* (box); *cerisier* (cherry tree); *chêne pubescent* (white oak); *chêne vert* (holm oak); *églantier* (wild rose); *épine blanche* (whitethorn); *épine noire* (blackthorn); *genévrier* (juniper); *pin sylvestre* (Scots pine); *viorne lantane* (wayfaring tree – *Viburnum lantana*).

Visiting time
Allow about 1.5hr to walk up to Puilaurens castle and back from the ticket office and to wander around the castle interior.

Further information
*   For Puilaurens castle: Accueil du château, 11140 Lapradelle-Puilaurens; tel: (00 33) (0)4 68 20 65 26; info@lapradelle-puilaurens.com; **www.lapradelle-puilaurens.com**.
*   The main walk is based on no 11 in the FFRP's *Topo-guide, Le Pays d'Axat... à pied* (2002; 8 Euros). The *sentier de découverte* is no 10 in that guide.
*   The nearest tourist office to Puilaurens castle is the Maison des Pyrénées du Pays Cathare, on the D117 to Quillan, about 5km west of Lapradelle, The FFRP *Topo-guide* can be bought there. Information about Puilaurens and other sites worth visiting in the region, and about accommodation and so on, can also be obtained there: Maison des Pyrénées du Pays Cathare, Rond-point d'Aliès, 11140 Axat; tel: (00 33) (0)4 68 20 59 61.

12 QUÉRIBUS

Two walks are described in this section.

The first is a long, hard, out-and-back route, starting from the town of Maury, south of Quéribus. It climbs rugged terrain and eventually reaches the ticket office a little way below the castle, before returning to Maury by the same route.

The route encounters steep slopes which cross sections of loose stones, and is not recommended when the ground is very wet, or for children at any time. Experienced and well-shod hillwalkers will enjoy the challenge, and the panoramas from the route are magnificent.

The harshness of the upper, wild, steep sections of the long walk contrast markedly with gentler, lower sections along tracks winding through carefully tended vineyards. One might even be tempted to regard this contrast as a metaphor for the stark dualism of Cathar thought.

A variant is offered, which follows the long walk up to Quéribus but then descends to Maury by a more direct route. That alternative descent involves a stretch of road walking.

The second, half-day walk is shorter and circular, starting from the village of Cucugnan, north of Quéribus, before climbing to the castle's ticket office, passing vineyards on the way. It then winds downhill, back to Cucugnan. It includes a long steep climb, but overall is only moderately strenuous.

CATHAR HISTORY: 1255

Quéribus castle is perched on a spike along a steep limestone ridge, and is possibly the most vertiginous of all the Cathar castles. On a clear day it can be seen from Perpignan, 25km to the southeast. Quéribus has often been described as the last of the Cathar fortresses to fall to the French, but that is – in part – misleading. It is true that a Cathar bishop was given shelter there after the Treaty of Paris in 1229, and that several Bons Hommes took refuge there around 1242. However, there is no record of any Cathar priests at Quéribus when the castle was besieged and finally surrendered to the French Crown in 1255.

Nevertheless, the defender of Quéribus in 1255 was a fervent Cathar supporter – one Chabert de Barbaira, a former military adviser to the King of Aragon. He had long since been dispossessed of his property in Languedoc by the crusade. He survived, took to the hills, established Quéribus as his base, and for over 20 years took part in guerrilla raids on French troops to the north.

The French were naturally eager to prise de Barbaira out of Quéribus. Despite their huge military strength in the region, they found this no easy task, and an attempt to besiege the castle in 1248 ended in failure. It was not until seven years later that Quéribus finally fell.

Later events

Soon afterwards Quéribus castle was considerably strengthened by the French king. Located very close to the border with Spain, it became a key frontier fortress. It was the scene of fighting in the 15th century and for a while was once again held by Spanish forces. But after the 17th century, when the frontier moved well to the south, the castle was left to crumble. Fortunately much of the fortifications remain and Quéribus now presents one of the most awe-inspiring sights in Cathar castle country.

PRACTICAL INFORMATION

Access to starting points

Maury lies along the main D117 between Perpignan and Quillan. There is a reasonably regular bus service to Maury from Perpignan. The summer tourist train between Rivesaltes (near Perpignan) and Axat also stops at Maury.

To travel by road to Cucugnan from Maury, turn off the D117 in Maury and head north on the D19. This road climbs to the Grau de Maury (from where another motor road, giving access to the Quéribus ticket office and car park, goes off on the right). It then descends, as the D123, to Cucugnan.

Navigation

The long walk is an amended version of a waymarked route from just outside Maury to Quéribus castle, opened in 2003. It has been amended to start from the town of Maury itself. The 'official' route begins at a car park adjacent to a picnic space (1), by the D19 at spot height 178, and signposted from there as 'de Maury à

Cucugnan'. The route is waymarked with yellow painted rectangles up to Quéribus castle.

The long walk starts in the centre of Maury (2), opposite the *mairie* (town hall). There are yellow waymarks along almost the whole route. It is best to ignore the first waymarks along the way (a local circuit which is not going to Quéribus) until, at point (4), you reach the 'official' route.

From Maury to Quéribus there are dozens of places where you have to fork right or left, or where other tracks and paths join from both sides. The waymarking is pretty good, but is designed for people climbing to Quéribus, not descending to Maury. If you plan to walk from Maury to Quéribus and return by the same route look closely at the various turnings on your way up. This will help you find the correct path on the way down.

The section of the long walk on the higher, steeper ground crosses some pretty rough country. Take care always to stay on the waymarked path.

The off-road sections of the variant down to Maury from Quéribus carry faint red and yellow waymarks.

The circular walk starts and finishes at the western end of Cucugnan, just below a restored windmill (14). It first follows the Sentier Cathare (waymarked blue and yellow). The return section, from Quéribus, is waymarked blue and yellow at first, but then – from point (18) – yellow and orange, back to Cucugnan.

Looking west from the top of the tower in Quéribus castle. Directly below is the Grau de Maury, a pass crossed by the road between Maury and Cucugnan.

153

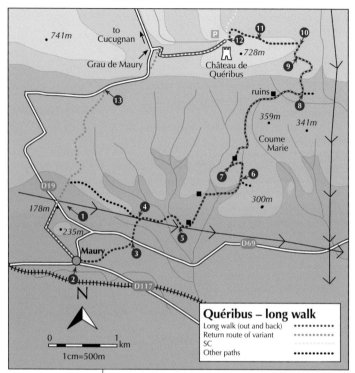

Quéribus – long walk

Long walk (out and back)	••••••••
Return route of variant	••••••••
SC	••••••••
Other paths	••••••••

ROUTE DESCRIPTION – LONG WALK AND VARIANT

Facing the mairie (town hall) in the centre of **Maury** (2), turn right and walk past the modern, geometric-shaped church, on your right. Soon start to descend steeply through the old part of the town, down the rue du 14 Juillet. On reaching the crossroads at the bottom of the slope go straight ahead, into the chemin de Saint-Roch.

This minor road takes you past a sports complex (right). Soon you see, above on the half-left, the handsome chapel of Saint-Roch. Keep to the road you are on, ignoring an access road to the chapel going up on the left. The road swings to the left and you are in open

Distances:	main walk 14km/8.7 miles (7km/4.3 miles out, 7km/4.3 miles back); variant 13km/8.1 miles (7km/4.3 miles out, 6km/3.7 miles back)
Time:	main walk 6.5hr (3.5hr ascent, 3hr return); variant 5.5hr (3.5hr ascent, 2hr return)
Altitude:	150m to 600m
Map:	IGN 1:25,000 2448OT (Thuir Ille-sur-Têt) ; Quéribus is in map fold 2A

country, passing stone walls on the left with blocks of limestone in several colours – grey, white, red and brown.

From here on, for a substantial section of the walk, vineyards occupy much of the terrain. Occasional signs on wooden boards reveal what kind of grape is being grown there, or give the name of the location. Others give information about trees (almond and mimosa in particular are not uncommon hereabouts). The little isolated, usually red-tiled, cabins of different shapes and sizes dotted around the vineyards are very photogenic.

The minor road climbs gently up a small valley. Near the top it swings to the left, and **Quéribus castle** comes into view straight ahead, perched impossibly on its rock pinnacle. The road goes down to meet the D69, running from left to right (3). Go straight across onto a jeep track directly opposite. ▶

Meet a track on the left; continue straight on, descend to cross a stream, then rise to another track junction where you fork right (4). From here on this is the 'official' route up to Quéribus, so follow the yellow waymarks carefully. Take another right fork and descend to cross a stream at a ford just after bending to the left and going under a power line. Ignore a track going off left, then go right at a fork shortly afterwards. Cross another little stream, this time over a bridge, then soon take a sharp left fork (5).

From (3) the next, short section of track is not on any waymarked walk, but is in an area to which, it seems, the public has access and over which you may go orienteering.

155

Quéribus castle: you can't miss it

The track climbs and curves around a small hill on your left. It bends left by a small cabin and power line, then comes to a dilapidated cabin by a pine tree. Follow the main track round to the right, ignoring tracks on the left. Go downhill a little to another stream course. Follow the waymarked track, which crosses that stream course then forks right. It then proceeds to climb the valley bottom of a small tributary stream. Come to a significant track fork (6) where signposts indicate waymarked routes straight ahead and to the right. Continue straight ahead up the valley bottom.

The track soon swings sharp left and climbs the other side of the valley. At the top the track forks three ways (7). Turn hard right to immediately pass a ruined stone building on the left. The track climbs, then bends left. From here you should have a stunning view of Quéribus castle straight ahead, looming hundreds of metres above you and looking completely unassailable. The track swings to the right, past beehives nestling among pine trees on the right. The track rises again, and swerves sharp left. By now you have left the vineyards almost entirely behind. The slopes of the steep valley on your right (the Coume Mairie) are covered in dense Mediterranean undergrowth.

Your track swings to the right. Take a right fork, then pass close to what looks like a large stone-built farmhouse – but which is, sadly, in ruins. Watch out carefully for the key turning point of the walk, about 300m after the ruins. Here you quit your near-level, well-made jeep track to take a rough track going steeply up the slope on your left (8).

The track soon becomes a narrow path, and remains unrelentingly steep for some time. The path is reasonably clear and well waymarked, but in one or two places may become a little faint. Keep checking off the waymarks carefully as you pass them so that you keep to the prescribed route. The ground here is steep, loose and slippery, and there are sheer cliffs on the right.

The path swings a little to the right, then zigzags straight up the slope. It follows the line of a minor spur in the hillside. The patches of bare limestone here are sharply serrated; be careful not to cut your hands and fingers. You come to a small section of drystone wall just below a rock spur jutting out to the left (don't go onto it in a strong wind). The views from that crag (9) are breathtaking: near-vertically to the jeep track you left to tackle this slope; an awesome limestone ravine cleaving the main ridge on the left; straight ahead over vineyards and hills to the Canigou massif and, further to the left, to the hazy Mediterranean coastline.

This view also has an interesting historical dimension. From here – and from other points on this walk – you may see, far to the south, the easternmost range of the Pyrenean mountains, rising to over 1200m and known as the Albères. They mark today's frontier between France and Spain. Just over three centuries ago that frontier moved to the Albères. It used to run near to where you stand now, close to an earlier border established when the French kingdom moved south during the crusade against the Cathars. At that time Quéribus and other Cathar castles assumed great military significance and were substantially strengthened or even completely rebuilt. But when the frontier was redrawn along the Albères in the 17th century, the castles lost their military importance and were left to fall into ruin.

Continue toiling up the steep path; eventually it swings right to reach the line of the ridge you have been aiming for. It then turns sharp left (10) to roughly follow the ridgeline, still climbing, but now much less steeply. The next section of the route may be a little disarming because, although you have now reached the ridge, the *sous-bois* (dense vegetation and low woodland) on either side only rarely affords a view of the surrounding countryside. Moreover, you are now walking on weathered limestone pavement, with great ankle-twisting potential. Relax not and keep a constant watch for the waymarks.

In due course the path swings right and emerges into more open country on the other side of the ridge (11). You now bear left. On the other side of the valley on your

Walkers descending from Quéribus castle

right the Sentier Cathare is terracing across the hillside, along a jeep track. In the far distance straight ahead you may be able to make out a high, lumpy ridge on which sits Peyrepertuse castle. Begin a fairly steep, long, downhill traverse of the slope, heading in the direction of Quéribus, even though that castle is not immediately in sight. Once again the path crosses a lot of spiky rock and sections of loose stones, so stay in 'mountain goat' mode.

Eventually the path descends to a patch of fairly level, semi-open ground. Quéribus castle now emerges close and massive on your left. Follow the path waymarks carefully across the semi-open ground, even though they seem to be taking you away from the castle. You soon meet a rough track, where you turn left. After another short distance, join the Sentier Cathare, on the right. Go through a metal gate by a cattle grid and, *enfin,* you have arrived at the ticket office at the foot of the access track to Quéribus castle (12).

Return to Maury by the same route – unless you are either continuing on foot to Cucugnan, or you want to take the alternative, more direct route back to Maury.

Variant

Follow the long walk as described from Maury to Quéribus.

For the return from the Quéribus ticket office, walk down the access road towards the Grau de Maury and the D123. Just before you reach the latter road, take a cut-off path on the left which crosses an area of scrub and meets the D123 where it bends to the right.

Walk down that road (now the D19) for about 500m. By a yellow signpost (13), turn left down a steep footpath. Where the path meets a track, go right, along that track. Go left at a track fork, then continue to follow the waymarked route downhill. In general, for most of the way aim to follow roughly the direction of a minor power line on wooden stakes which is descending towards Maury.

Your route winds through an area of vineyards and then approaches a pine forest. Shortly after entering that, fork right. On leaving the forest, descend steeply across open country towards a car park (1). Just beyond that is the D19 road; cross over and follow the minor road opposite. It bends to the left and enters Maury.

ROUTE DESCRIPTION – CIRCULAR WALK

Distance:	12km (7.4 miles)
Time:	3.5hr
Altitude:	260m to 600m
Map:	IGN 1:25,000 2447 OT (Tuchan); Quéribus is in map fold 6D

This walk starts and finishes at the western end of **Cucugnan** village, just below the restored windmill (14). Walk through Cucugnan to its far eastern end, following the waymarked route of the Sentier Cathare. Descend a steep road at the eastern end of the village from where you can see **Quéribus castle** in the distance high above. Meet the D14 (15), which bypasses the village. Cross that road and take a minor motor road on the other side, almost directly opposite.

After a very short distance, turn right at a road crossing. The road bends to the left with vineyards on either side. Ignore tracks going off to the right until you come to a T-junction with a clump of conifer trees on the left. Here turn right onto a dirt track (16). That track descends a little way to cross a stream, then starts to climb gradually. The soil in places is almost bright orange. The vineyards become sparser, and on both sides of the track there is now mostly dry, scented Mediterranean scrub. Pass a smallholding on the right. Near the head of the valley you are following the track turns sharp left and becomes a path (17). Follow that.

At first the path climbs gradually, but then, as it bears to the right and enters low woodland, climbs quite steeply for some while. The ground is rocky in places, and can be slippery after rainfall, so take great care. From various places there are, to the left, fine views over Cucugnan below and, in the far distance, the huge, irregular-shaped profile of the limestone cliffs on which the remains of Peyrepertuse castle are perched.

At last the slope levels out. Your path bears to the right and twists and turns with dark shrubs on either side. (If you have ever walked through the maze at Hampton Court, you may now be reminded of that experience.) You won't get lost as long as you keep to the waymarked path.

Finally, reach some open ground from where there is a magnificent view of Quéribus castle straight ahead. It may be a cliché to say that Cathar castles seem to grow out of the very rock on which they are poised, but Quéribus does give this impression – especially when the sun is behind it and it is difficult to distinguish between the rock pinnacle and the castle.

Descend the track ahead, past a car park and down to the ticket office at the entrance to the castle (12).

The return to Cucugnan is less steep. From just below the Quéribus ticket office, with the car park rising up the slope ahead of you, take the track going off to the right, on the level, with wooden shacks (WCs) to the right of the track.

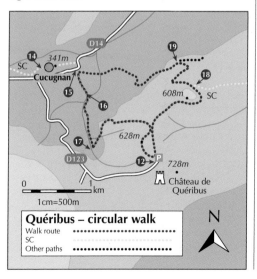

Quéribus – circular walk

Walk route •
SC
Other paths •

N

Follow that track (still the Sentier Cathare) as it contours to the right, later bears left, then comes to a track junction (18). En route you may have to pass through metal gates at the side of cattle grids. Beware: there may be electrified fences on either side.

Turn left at the junction. The waymarking from here changes from the yellow and blue of the Sentier Cathare to yellow and orange. After a little way, at a fine viewpoint, follow your track as it turns sharp right. In due course the track swings to the left, descends quite steeply, then meets a tarmacked lane (19).

Turn left. The lane winds gently across the side of a hill; reaches flatter country; crosses a streambed; then joins your outward route. Turn right there to reach the D14 (15). Cross that road and climb the hill ahead, back into Cucugnan.

POINTS OF INTEREST

Maury: This little town has a mixture of older stone buildings and starker, more modern edifices, including the town hall. It is utterly dedicated to the wine trade. A leaflet lists no fewer than 21 places in and around the town where you can indulge in wine tasting. This region is particularly well known for its fortified wines and dessert wines.

Quéribus castle: There is some very well-preserved vaulting inside this fortress and, from the top of the tower, a stunning panorama. The whole structure is surprisingly large, given how little ground there is on which to build. The castle is closed for much of January; otherwise open throughout the year (though sometimes closed at short notice if the strength of the wind renders walking around the castle dangerous). The entry ticket also gives free entry to the theatre in Cucugnan. There is a climb of about 80m from Quéribus ticket office to the castle.

Cucugnan: This attractive tourist village has benefited perhaps more than any other from being close to Cathar castles. Mostly free of motor traffic, it has several craft shops and wine-tasting centres; its neo-gothic church is open to visitors; and there are guided tours to its restored windmill. It also has a 'pocket theatre' (the Théâtre Achille Mir), named after a local 19th-century writer. He wrote a story in Occitan of a sermon about hellfire and damnation given by the curé of Cucugnan to his wayward, pleasure-loving flock. Alphonse Daudet subsequently wrote a French version of the story, widely known in France. An intriguing 20min presentation of the story is shown in the theatre; continuous performances throughout the year except in January.

Visiting times
To walk up to Quéribus castle from the ticket office and back, and to tour the castle, allow at least 1hr.

Maury and Cucugnan are also both worth exploring and in both cases allow at least 2hr. Allow another 30min in Cucugnan if you also watch the presentation of 'the curé's sermon' in the village's small theatre.

Further information
- The long walk is based on one in a leaflet-cum-postcard entitled *Rando: de Maury à Cucugnan via le château de Quéribus* and obtained from the mairie of Maury:
- Mairie de Maury, 66460 Maury; tel: (00 33) (0)4 68 59 15 24; mairie.maury@wanadoo.fr.
- The circular walk is in *Rando Découvertes en famille*, a booklet of local walks, price 8 Euros, available locally.
- For more information about Quéribus castle and Cucugnan: Mairie de Cucugnan, 11350 Cucugnan; tel: (00 33) (0)4 68 45 03 69; mairie.cucugnan@free.fr; **mairie.cucugnan.free.fr**.
- At the time of writing a new tourist office is being opened to cover several communes in this district: L'Office Intercommunal de Tourisme des Hautes Corbières, Route de Padern, 11350 Cucugnan; tel: (00 33) (0)4 68 45 69 40; ot-hautescorbieres.com.

13 PEYREPERTUSE

Two walks – a long and a short one – are offered in this section, both within sight of Peyrepertuse castle. Both start from the village of Duilhac-sous-Peyrepertuse which, as its name implies, is located directly below the castle. The surrounding high, *garrigue*-covered limestone hills and cliffs make for a dramatic landscape.

Both walks can be combined with a visit to the castle but, given the castle's size and location, such a visit demands a good deal of time and energy.

The long walk is an out-and-back route, and partly follows the Sentier Cathare. It leaves that long-distance path to climb to the magnificent summit of La Quille (964m), a limestone ridge above and directly opposite Peyrepertuse castle.

A variant of the long walk involves a longer descent via the Pla de St-Paul, from where there is another magnificent panorama.

The short walk is a circular route passing close to a popular beauty spot, the Moulin de Ribaute – a former mill on the sparkling River Verdouble.

CATHAR HISTORY: 1258

Within no great distance of Quéribus – and likewise almost floating high on limestone cliffs – are the remains of Peyrepertuse castle.

Until 1240 the castle played no great part in the history of the crusade against the Cathars. It was another bastion of Cathar support, occupied for most of the period by Guilhem de Peyrepertuse, twice ex-communicated by the Pope for his opposition to the crusade. However, the castle's remoteness and formidable natural defences for long dissuaded French military leaders from trying to take it by force.

But in 1240 Guilhem de Peyrepertuse took part in an audacious attempt led by the son of the former Viscount of Carcassonne to recover that city from the French. When that attempt failed, the assailants fled southwards towards the Pyrenees. French troops pursued them and, in so doing, lay siege to Peyrepertuse. Caught at the beginning of winter without supplies or hope of receiving military support, Guilhem de Peyrepertuse surrendered the castle to the French. It became a royal fortress and was almost completely rebuilt from around 1250, part of the chain of French fortresses along the frontier with Spain.

Peyrepertuse – with other nearby castles such as Puilaurens and Quéribus – passed definitively to the French Crown with the Treaty of Corbeil in 1258. This treaty, made between Louis IX of France and Jaume I of Aragon, was drawn up to establish a clear frontier between the two kingdoms. It ran across a region over which the two powers had fought for generations. It also sealed the success of the French military campaign to seize control of Languedoc, which had effectively begun nearly 50 years earlier with the massacre at Béziers.

Above Peyrepertuse castle, with the hills of the Corbières region in the distance

Later events

The Treaty of Corbeil did not mark a final peace between France and its southern neighbours. Conflicts between French and Spanish forces continued in this frontier zone during the following 400 years. When the frontier moved further south in the 17th century Peyrepertuse lost its military significance and thereafter fell into ruin. However, it was designated an historic monument in 1908, and since 1977 has been the site of important archaeological investigations. A picture of the castle appeared on a French postage stamp in 2004.

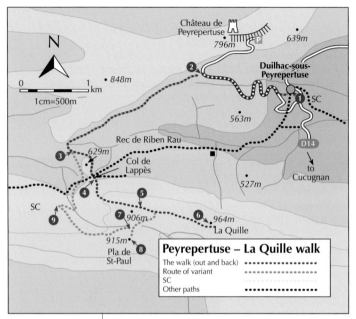

Peyrepertuse – La Quille walk

The walk (out and back)	●●●●●●●●●●●●
Route of variant	●●●●●●●●●●●●
SC	●●●●●●●●●●●●
Other paths	●●●●●●●●●●●●

PRACTICAL INFORMATION

Access to starting point

To reach Duilhac by road from Maury, take the D19 heading north, go through a pass – the Grau de Maury – and descend (by the same road, now the D123) towards Cucugnan. Just before that village, turn left onto the D14 and follow that to Duilhac.

Public transport in this area is scarce.

Navigation

La Quille walk: between points (1) and (2), follow the blue and yellow waymarks of the Sentier Cathare. These continue up to point (3), but are joined at point (2) by the red and white waymarks of the GR36. Between points (3) and (5) there are no waymarks; follow the directions given below carefully. Shortly after point (5) occasional yellow waymarks indicate the route to the summit.

Variant via the Pla de St-Paul: indicated for most of the way between points (6) and (9) by yellow waymarks. From (9) to the end of the walk follow the blue and yellow waymarks of the Sentier Cathare. The return route between points (7) and (9) is steep in places, and may be muddy and slippery in wet weather.

The Moulin de Ribaute route is indicated throughout by yellow waymarks.

ROUTE DESCRIPTION – LONG (LA QUILLE) WALK AND VARIANT

Distances:	main walk 14km/8.7 miles (7km/4.3 miles out, 7km/4.3 miles back); variant 16km/9.9 miles (7km/4.3 miles out, 9km/5.6 miles back)
Time:	main walk 5.5hr (3hr ascent, 2.5hr return); variant 6.5hr (3hr ascent, 3.5hr return)
Altitude:	300m to 964m
Map:	IGN 1:25,000 2447OT (Tuchan); Peyrepertuse castle is in map fold 5C; Duilhac-sous-Peyrepertuse is in map fold 5D

This walk starts at the Auberge du Vieux Moulin in the lower part of **Duilhac-sous-Peyrepertuse**, on the D14 (1). Follow the Sentier Cathare waymarks up through the village. Bear right. Pass the village church, towering above you on the right. Turn left, then right, and follow the street ahead out of the village. Meet the tarmacked access road to Peyrepertuse castle just to the right of a pizzeria; turn right there.

The Sentier Cathare climbs that winding access road for 2km (cut-off paths exist, but are not waymarked). Peyrepertuse castle is perched on the massive cliffs to your right.

The high, open plateau of La Quille

From (2): if you want to visit the castle, turn right up the access road. Return to this point after your visit.

Eventually the access road to the castle swings sharply to the right (2), while the Sentier Cathare continues straight on, along a jeep track heading west. ◀

Follow the jeep track westwards for 2.5km as it terraces high above the valley of the Rec de Riben Rau, on your left (the GR36 also follows this route). On the other side of the valley towers the rugged limestone crest of La Quille (which you are heading for). Where the track finally reaches the head of the valley, it bends to the left. To the right is a good view of the east face of the Pech de Bugarach.

You will soon see on the half-right that the GR36 and the Sentier Cathare are waymarked to leave the track and go through a gap in a fence on the right (3). Ignore that turning and keep on the track as it heads east, passes to the left of a small wooded hill, then bends to the right. Reach a T-junction of tracks at the Col de Lappès (4).

Go straight ahead up a grass slope, then cross a fence by a gap-stile a few metres beyond, on the edge of an area of woodland. The path from here weaves and climbs through mostly dense woodland with a few clearings. At first it is not waymarked, although there are occasional stone cairns. It is easy to lose the path where it meets an area of pine trees not long after you leave the track at the col. Here, go straight up the steep slope on the left. The path soon reappears, as it bends to the right.

After passing across semi-open ground, the path's direction becomes more easterly (that is, it swings left and climbs very steeply, with a small, narrow valley on the right). Eventually the steepness eases and the dense woodland gives way to more scattered vegetation. The higher you go the more the view opens up. Soon you see a distinct hill on the right (at 906m). As you approach the left side of that hill, emerge onto a limestone plateau where, for much of the year, there is an abundance of small, colourful wild flowers.

As you pass the hill on your right, the path descends a little to the top of a dry valley (5). The impressive crest of La Quille is now ahead, slightly to the left.

The path rises again on the left-hand slope of the dry valley and runs diagonally across the slope, roughly parallel to the crest of the ridge on the left. At first the line is clear enough, but becomes more difficult to follow later on, especially as it forks quite a lot. Keep a little to the right of the ridge, just below the scrub covering the crest of the hill.

Pass close by a gap on the left, between two lime-stone crags in the ridge. The scrub is rapidly obscuring what must have been an impressive view towards Peyrepertuse castle.

Take care now as you cross more open ground to head for a single pine tree. Look out too for yellow waymarks on outcrops of limestone in the ground which indicate the route. If in doubt, keep forking left where the path divides. If you manage to keep to the path you eventually come out on the crest of the ridge at a point about halfway between the gap between the limestone crags and a grassy plateau at the head of another small valley, on your right.

It is not until you actually reach this point on the ridge (6) that you realise it is the highest point (La Quille, 964m). It is a stretch of scrub-covered limestone pave-ment which plunges almost vertically to the north and

Inside Peyrepertuse, one of the biggest of the Cathar castles

which commands a magnificent view across to Peyrepertuse castle, down to Duilhac village, and over the surrounding dramatic landscape of limestone ridges and deeply incised valleys – a great place for lunch.

Return to Duilhac by the same route.

Variant (return via the Pla de St-Paul)

Climb to La Quille by the route described above.

For the return, retrace your steps alongside the crest of the ridge, towards the hill at 906m. Instead of going to the right of that hill, pass to its left. Head for a col (7) lying between that hill and the Pla de St-Paul further over on the left.

From the col, turn left and climb to the top of the Pla de St-Paul (8). There is a magnificent view from there over the long, deep east–west valley in which lies St-Paul-de-Fenouillet, almost immediately below. Further to the south lie the Fenouillèdes hills and, beyond that, Canigou mountain. Far to the left you may be able to see the Mediterranean coastline.

Go back down to the col and pick up a path indicated by yellow waymarks, descending a valley on the left. The path is a little unclear at first, but as it enters low woodland and descends more steeply, becomes quite obvious. It is waymarked all the way down to the upper (right-hand) part of a flattish area of open ground (9), where you can pick up the Sentier Cathare. Turn right and follow the Sentier Cathare as it almost immediately leaves the open area and descends steeply into a wooded valley to the right.

The path passes beneath limestone crags. It then swings to the left and eventually passes below a watering point for livestock. Immediately after that it meets a jeep track. Turn right along that track for a very few metres. Then turn left off the track to follow the Sentier Cathare as it descends a little more, then terraces around the head of a valley which falls away on your left.

Pass through a gap in a fence and meet another jeep track (3) – the track you followed on your way out. Turn left and follow that track. It bears right, around the head of the valley on the right. Retrace your steps all the way back to Duilhac.

ROUTE DESCRIPTION – SHORT (MOULIN DE RIBAUTE) WALK

Distances:	5km (3.1 miles)
Time:	2.5hr
Altitude:	230m to 400m
Map:	as for long walk

On the D14 through **Duilhac-sous-Peyrepertuse**, just below the Auberge du Vieux Moulin, there is a

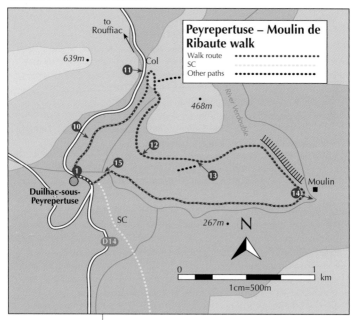

mapboard showing the route (1). Take the narrow lane descending from the road to the left of the mapboard, with small, cultivated terraces just below. The lane becomes a jeep track, swings right to cross a stream, then climbs gently on the other side. This track runs roughly parallel to the D14, above on the left. You will walk below and parallel to that road all the way to the col at the highest point on this walk.

Shortly after passing some olive trees on the right, take a footpath waymarked as going off the track on the left (10). The surface of the path is almost flat, bare rock. After passing through a shady section, the path emerges into the open. It crosses more flat, bare rock, where the line of the path becomes less clear, so follow the waymarking with care. The path zigzags up the slope on the left, then soon afterwards climbs a short steep section to emerge onto the D14 (11).

Turn off the road immediately to the right. You are now at the Col de la Croix dessus. Take the gravel track going off on the right, where there is a signpost for the Moulin de Ribaute. The track soon becomes a dirt track; it swings to the left, then forks. Take the right fork. You have a very fine view back down to Duilhac, now straight ahead. The crags and towers of **Peyrepertuse castle** are high above, on your right.

The vegetation here is conifer trees and low ever-green oak. The track winds gradually downhill. After passing below a limestone crag, the track swings sharp left (12). A little further on, the track itself turns sharp right (13). Be careful to carry straight on, along a stony path.

The path climbs a little, then emerges high above the gorge of the Verdouble river, on the left. The path now bends right and runs steeply downhill, parallel to the deep valley on the left. The bare limestone on the path may be slippery after rain.

Where the path reaches the bottom of the hill, by some ruined stone buildings, it is waymarked to go right. But turn left here (you will return to this point shortly) to emerge very quickly in a delightful open area by the Verdouble river. On the other side of the river are the substantial remains of the **Moulin de Ribaute** (14).

Return to the waymarked path and follow it back in the direction of Duilhac. You are close to the bottom of a small valley, which leads back to the village. The path is very clear and passes through a mixture of woodland and open ground. At one point it crosses a vineyard; aim for its far left-hand corner.

A little further on – as the hill on the left gives way to flatter ground – the path climbs a little and Duilhac comes into sight once again, straight ahead. So too do the magnificent cliffs on which Peyrepertuse castle are perched.

The path swings to the left to cross a couple of streams (15). There is an old iron girder to help you across the second one, but paddling should not be too uncomfort-able. The path climbs a little on the other side of the stream, with open ground on the left. With the D14 just above on the right, the path joins a track followed by the Sentier Cathare. Follow the track as it winds uphill and soon meets the D14. Turn right, and the starting point (1) is a little further along that road.

POINTS OF INTEREST

Duilhac-sous-Peyrepertuse: This village has several attractive features, including its restored church (once part of a small medieval fort), and the Vieux Moulin ('old mill') restaurant, in a former olive oil mill. But its most striking feature is a powerful spring in a rock face next to the restaurant, from which delicious fresh water tumbles into a canal. An engraving by the spring says 'May whoever drinks here fall in love'.

Peyrepertuse castle: The buildings and walls of this castle are strung out along a limestone ridge, with steep cliffs on nearly all sides. From a distance the ridge looks like part of a gigantic fossil jawbone, with a monstrous isolated molar tooth at one end. The castle ruins extend over a much larger area than those of Quéribus, and is the largest of the Corbières fortresses.

The Sentier Cathare passes south of the castle, but the GR36 long-distance path actually goes through the ticket office. In *Clear Waters Rising* Nicholas Crane describes how, one September night on his trek north along the GR36, he slept rough in the castle. 'I lay looking up at the square of stars above the ruined walls,' he wrote, 'sure that I could smell the lamp fat and greasy leather of medieval soldiery.'

The castle is open every day throughout the year, except in January. It may be closed at short notice in stormy conditions.

The Moulin de Ribaute: The remains of this former flour mill on the River Verdouble are in an idyllic location. The 'no bathing' sign painted on its wall is more honoured in the breach than the observance – in both senses of that phrase. On a hot summer's day the temptation to bathe or paddle in the deep rock pools above the mill is irresistible – and indeed, the crystal-clear river would be dishonoured were that temptation to be resisted.

Visiting times

Starting from the Peyrepertuse castle ticket office, allow at least 1.5hr to walk up to the castle entrance and back and to stroll around the remains of this huge, clifftop fortification. Be careful if you reach the very highest point within the castle walls, especially in windy conditions, as there are unfenced sheer drops on most sides.

If you tackle the long walk up to La Quille, and add to your outward journey a visit to Peyrepertuse castle, be prepared for a long, physically demanding day. Allow 2.5hr to walk up to the castle and back from point (2) and to explore the castle itself.

If you tackle the short walk, then also walk up to Peyrepertuse castle and back from Duilhac (and visit the castle), allow at least 3hr for that round trip between village and castle. (If you have a motor vehicle you could drive up the access road to the castle from Duilhac, rather than walk.)

Further information

*   The long (La Quille) walk is based on one in a locally available book of walks, *Randonnées en Pays Cathare* by Jacques Jolfre (Rando Éditions, 2002). The short (Moulin de Ribaute) walk is in *Rando Découvertes en famille* (see Quéribus, section 12).
*   For information about Peyrepertuse castle and Duilhac, contact the Duilhac *mairie* at Chemin du Fort, 11350 Duilhac-sous-Peyrepertuse; tel: (00 33) (0)4 68 45 40 55; mairie.duilhac@wanadoo.fr; **www.chateau-peyrepertuse.com**.
*   For information about the castle, and to make bookings for guided tours, tel: (00 33) (0)6 71 58 63 36; chateau.peyrepertuse@wanadoo.fr.
*   At the time of writing, a new tourist office is being opened to cover several communes in this district: L'Office Intercommunal de Tourisme des Hautes Corbières, Route de Padern, 11350 Cucugnan; tel: (00 33) (0)4 68 45 69 40; ot-hautescorbieres.com.

14 VILLEROUGE-TERMENÈS

After approaching Carcassonne from the north and passing through that city, the GR36 long-distance footpath heads east, then turns south to cross the Corbières hills. Just outside the town of Lagrasse, famous for its once-powerful Benedictine abbey, the path divides. The western arm, the GR36A, passes close to the remains of Termes castle. The eastern arm, the GR36B, crosses the splendid limestone massif of the Serre de Blanes and descends to Villerouge-Termenès. Both arms continue southwards and meet up before reaching Peyrepertuse castle. An east–west footpath between Villerouge-Termenès and Termes links the GR36A and the GR36B and is called, not surprisingly, the GR36AB.

Two out-and-back walks are described below, both starting from Villerouge-Termenès and following sections of these long-distance paths. They cross and offer views over the Corbières hills, on whose lower slopes are vineyards producing grapes for delectable Corbières wine.

The shorter walk goes north, up to Mont Major, the highest point on the Serre de Blanes. This is a very good half-day hill walk, mostly in open country covered by wild Mediterranean vegetation.

The second walk follows the GR36AB all the way to Termes castle and back. This is a long walk which can be very tiring, even for fit walkers – especially if you aim to visit both castles on the same day. It is, however, extremely rewarding. Some of the route is in open country from where there are excellent views, but long sections also pass through forest, where the shade will be welcome on a hot day.

CATHAR HISTORY: 1321

From about the middle of the 13th century the remaining Cathars no longer had any fortresses in the region to which they could flee for safety. Few in number, hunted, penniless, they nevertheless managed to survive, darting between hiding places.

Among the rural population in the hills and mountains south of Foix, the Cathar faith enjoyed a remarkable resurgence under Pierre Authié in the early 14th century (see Lordat and Montaillou, sections 6 and 7). However, it ended with the execution of Authié and a number of his companions in 1310.

The faint embers of the Cathar faith in Languedoc were finally doused when the last of the Languedoc *Bons Hommes*, Guillaume Bélibaste, was burnt at the stake in the autumn of 1321. This execution was carried out in the grounds of the castle of Villerouge-Termenès, hidden away in the back country of the Corbières.

A peasant farmer from the Corbières country, Bélibaste's links with the Authié community are not entirely clear. However, it seems he was ordained by one of Authié's followers after he sought atonement for murdering a shepherd during a quarrel.

Although Bélibaste was imprisoned in Carcassonne, he escaped in 1309. He fled south to Catalunya, where he was welcomed by other Cathar believers who had taken refuge south of the Pyrenees. Being the only ordained Cathar minister among them, Bélibaste became the leader of that small Cathar community.

Bélibaste never lost his taste for wealth and pleasures of the flesh. He lived with a woman who became pregnant by him and, in 1320, was lured back to France by a bounty hunter's phoney promise of financial gain.

Villerouge-Termenès castle. The Serre de Blanes walk climbs the open slope in the background.

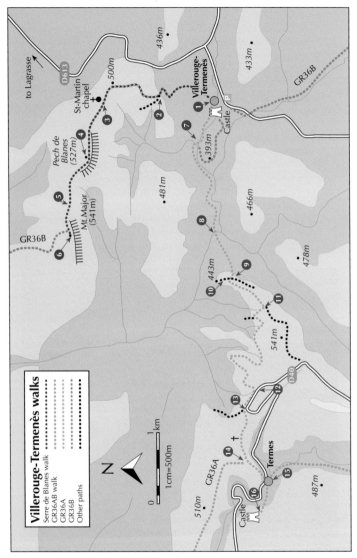

Villerouge-Termenès walks

Serre de Blanes walk
GR36AB walk
GR36A
GR36B
Other paths

N

0   1cm=500m

0   1 km

Bélibaste was caught and handed over to his feudal lord the Archbishop of Narbonne, who also owned Villerouge-Termenès castle. Bélibaste was tried and executed in his native country, the Corbières

Later events
The castle in which this awful sentence was carried out is remarkably well preserved. Villerouge-Termenès was taken by Simon de Montfort without a fight in 1210.

The castle miraculously survived the centuries without being demolished or pillaged, unlike so many others in Cathar castle country. It has been substantially restored in recent times and is being developed as a tourist attraction of some dimension.

Termes castle
The remains of Termes castle, at the far end of the second walk, bring us back in time to almost the beginning of the crusade against the Cathars. For it was in 1210 that Termes was beseiged by de Montfort's forces. The castle's defenders were eventually forced to make a desperate dash for freedom after rats infected their water supply. However, most were caught and slaughtered by the French, who then took control of the castle. Termes was eventually demolished by order of the French Crown in 1653.

PRACTICAL INFORMATION
Access to starting points
Villerouge-Termenès lies on the D613, the principal road across the Corbières. That road runs from Couiza in the Aude valley, a little north of Quillan, northeast to Narbonne. From Lagrasse, to the north, go south on the D3, then turn right onto the D23. That road eventually meets the D613, where you turn right for Villerouge-Termenès.

Public transport is very scarce in this area.

Navigation
Except for a couple of short sections, the entire routes of both walks are indicated by red and white waymarks. Those short sections present no navigation problems and are explained in the route descriptions. However, note in particular that the first part of the GR36AB walk out

of Villerouge-Termenès does not follow the *waymarked* GR36AB but follows a tarmacked lane which is met by the GR36AB after a short distance.

Note also that there is a river crossing at point (8) on the GR36AB walk which may be difficult in winter and impossible during or after heavy rainfall.

You may see a few other waymarks, including possibly some faded red and yellow ones – ignore them.

ROUTE DESCRIPTION – SERRE DE BLANES WALK

Distance:	9km (5.6 miles)
Time:	3hr
Altitude:	320m to 541m
Map:	IGN 1:25,000 2446O (Capendu) and 2447OT (Tuchan); Villerouge-Termenès is in map fold 7A of the Tuchan map

From the principal footbridge over the stream in **Villerouge-Termenès** (1), facing and just below the castle, bear to the right, with a stream on your right. After bearing left climb up through the village, following the red and white waymarks of the GR36B. Go straight ahead at a street crossing and soon emerge in the countryside above Villerouge-Termenès. Just beyond the village, to the right and left of your track, are the remains of former windmills.

Keep to the waymarked track, ignoring others going off on either side. As your track approaches the hills ahead, it swings left, then sharply right, then left again.

Soon afterwards you reach a small col (2). The impressive south-facing cliffs of the Serre de Blanes are now in full view straight ahead. You are aiming for the highest point, Mont Major, towards the far western end of the hill.

At the col, turn off the track to follow the clearly defined, waymarked path which climbs up the shoulder of the slope on the right. Follow this path for the rest of the ascent through Mediterranean vegetation with a remarkable variety of colourful and often scented herbs, flowers and other plants.

The path climbs steadily towards the main ridgeline.

From the ridgeline – and for the rest of the walk over to Mont Major – there are, on a clear day, fabulous views in all directions. In particular, the eastern Pyrenees mountains are on the southern horizon and the Montagne Noire defines the horizon to the north. To the east stretch the coastal lowlands. Closer on all sides are the rolling hills of the Corbières region; to the southwest is the unmistakable jagged profile of the Pech de Bugarach.

The path swings to the left and descends. From here it follows the ridgeline all the way to Mont Major. Ignore less well-defined paths which descend the slope to the right. Your path (the GR36B) first goes down to a col where the small chapel of Saint-Martin stands (3). Restoration work has been carried out here recently, and it may serve as a useful shelter if the weather suddenly becomes inclement.

Walker on the Serre de Blane, near Villerouge-Termenès (the building on the left is the Saint-Martin chapel)

Pass to the left of the chapel and follow the path up the steep slope ahead. The highest point on the plateau above is the Pech de Blanes (4). From there the path descends again and eventually reaches another col (5). There is then another climb, very steep at first and possibly quite slippery in wet conditions. The slope finally eases. The GR36B turns off to descend to the right. But continue straight on for a short distance to reach the highest point, Mont Major (6) – the second of the two mounds reached after the climb from the col.

From the cliffs of Mont Major look down upon Villerouge-Termenès, tucked into a valley below. Looking north from the highest point you may be able to pick out the bulky grey tower of Lagrasse Abbey about 7km away.

Return to Villerouge-Termenès by the same route. ◀

The GR36B winds down to Lagrasse, climbs the impressive limestone massif beyond (the Montagne d'Alaric), then heads west over high ground, before descending towards Carcassone.

ROUTE DESCRIPTION – GR36AB WALK

Distance:	16km (9.9 miles)
Time:	6hr
Altitude:	320m to 480m
Map:	IGN 1:25,000 2447OT (Tuchan); Villerouge-Termenès is in map fold 7A

Note: Don't take the GR36AB out of **Villerouge-Termenès**: it climbs the 393m hill (Pech Rigaud on the 1:25,000 map), then comes down again not far from the start. It's a scenic route, but it is wiser to conserve your time and energy for the long walk ahead by following the unwaymarked cut-off described below.

From the main entrance to the castle in the village (1), facing a yellow post-box, go left up a village street. It curves left, then right, and comes to street junction near the top corner of the village. Take the tarmacked road going slightly downhill on the left. A fine view of the west face of the castle soon appears on the left, just across a vineyard.

The road curves to the right, passes a pink house on the left, and goes down a small valley. It crosses a streambed on the right (7), where the GR36AB joins this route from the left. Go past a small chapel, on the left. The road becomes a track. ▶

The valley narrows to a mini-gorge and the track becomes a path. The trail rises a little and reaches a ruined stone building. Go down on the right to a stream (8).

Cross that stream and take a path going up into dense low woodland ahead. After a long, steady climb, emerge onto an open track (9). Turn right there. Shortly afterwards, follow the track round a sharp left bend.

On the right, a rough path goes up to point 443 (10); a crow's nest hill on a bare limestone pavement with a marvellous panorama over the surrounding countryside.

After the sharp left bend, follow the track along the line of the semi-open ridge. There are fire lookout posts in trees nearby.

At a track fork (11), turn right. Take a left fork soon afterwards. The route now becomes a balcony forest walk roughly along a line of springs, with occasional great views to the north. At the first stream crossing, the track becomes a path. That path winds for a long way to the left and right. Later it climbs, becomes a rough track, then meets the D40 (12).

Turn right and follow that road for a little way. Go straight ahead at a col where the road turns sharp left (13). Follow the track beyond, down to an iron cross on a large stone plinth. From about here the remains of **Termes castle** come into view ahead. Where the track turns sharp left, continue straight ahead on a stony path, going downhill.

At a small col where you meet the GR36A coming from the right (14), continue downhill, straight ahead.

Not long after you enter the charming village of Termes (15), with its flower-decked bridges. A building on the other side of the river beyond a bridge serves as the ticket office for Termes castle. It also has an

At the time this walk was surveyed, the track after the chapel was being widened and lengthened. It may now extend further down the valley.

Termes village – a pretty and tranquil little settlement, tucked away in the Corbières hills

interesting exhibition (in French) on the history of the Cathars and Termes castle.

Leave the GR36A here, but the route up to the castle (16) from the ticket office is obvious.

From Termes castle, return by your long outward route all the way back to Villerouge-Termenès.

POINTS OF INTEREST

Villerouge-Termenès castle: You can wander from room to room inside this square-shaped castle; you can also go out along the ramparts. There are videos, displays and other original devices to make you feel that you are back in the 14th century, at the time of poor Bélibaste's detention. Part of the castle is now a restaurant, la Rôtisserie Médiévale, serving medieval dishes. The castle is open from April to mid-October; in February and March it is open at weekends and during school holidays.

Termes castle: Much less remains of this fortification, but what does is being well conserved. The castle still holds much of interest for those fascinated by medieval military architecture. It is open from April to mid-October; from mid-October to mid-December it is open at weekends and during school holidays.

Visiting times
Allow at least 1hr to visit Villerouge-Termenès castle. If you stay for one of their medieval feasts, allow a great deal longer (including recovery time).

A walk around the hilltop remains of Termes castle would take you about 30min, but the viewpoint is so magnificent that it is best not hurried.

Further information
- At the time of writing there is no published guide to the GR36 long-distance path. However, the routes of both walks form part of a two-day tour linking Villerouge-Termenès, Termes and Lagrasse, walk 30 in the FFRP's *Topo-guide, L'Aude, Pays Cathare à pied* (2000) (see Appendix 2).
- Le Château, 11330 Villerouge-Termenès; tel: (00 33) (0)4 68 70 09 11/(0)4 68 70 04 89; chateau.villerouge@wanadoo.fr; **www.aude-tourisme.com/chateauVillerouge.**
- Château de Termes, 11330 Termes; tel: (00 33) (0)4 68 70 09 20; chateau.termes@wanadoo.fr; **www.audetourisme.com/chateauTermes**.

15 RENNES-LE-CHÂTEAU

This section covers a circular walk starting from the town of Couiza, north of Quillan in the Aude valley, and takes about 4hr. The route ascends to Rennes-le-Château, descends to Coustaussa, and passes close to old stone cabins known as *capitelles* before returning to Couiza. The landscape is a mixture of woodland, fields and limestone plateau.

Prominent to the south at many stages along the route is the huge and (for hillwalkers) extremely inviting Pech de Bugarach.

CATHAR HISTORY: 1891

The hilltop village of Rennes-le-Château is situated on a plateau above the Aude valley, about 30km south of Carcassonne. The Visigoths established a powerful stronghold, and in 1210 Simon de Montfort largely destroyed a castle here.

The village is most famous for its legend of secret treasure allegedly discovered in the late 19th century by the village priest, Bérenger Saunière.

Saunière was the parish priest from 1885 until his death in 1917. From 1891 onwards he undertook substantial restoration work on the parish church. He also created the nearby garden, the neo-gothic Magdala tower and the opulent Villa Béthania. He and his housekeeper Marie Denarnaud adopted a lavish lifestyle.

One theory is that Saunière financed all this after discovering Cathar treasure, smuggled out of Montségur just before its capitulation and hidden in the churchyard at Rennes-le-Château. There is no shortage of alternative theories, including some which revolve around Visigoth treasure, the Holy Grail and plundered gold. The real source (or sources) of Saunière's wealth has not yet been conclusively established.

PRACTICAL INFORMATION
Access to starting point
Couiza lies along the D118, the main north–south road along the Aude valley, between Carcassonne and Quillan. Bus and train services along the Aude valley pass through Couiza.

Looking down on Couiza, where the walk to Rennes-le-Château begins

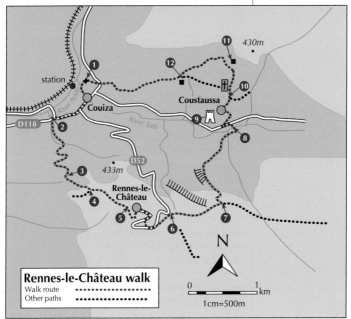

Rennes-le-Château walk

Walk route ••••••••••••••••
Other paths ••••••••••••••••

0   1 km

1cm=500m

Navigation

The yellow waymarks of a local path circuit indicate a walk from Couiza (1) up to Rennes-le-Château (5). There follows a section along a minor road to point (7). Much of the downhill section between points (7) and (8) is waymarked with large, homemade, red-and-white signs. The yellow waymarks of another local circuit show the route from near Coustaussa back to Couiza.

ROUTE DESCRIPTION

Distance:	11km (6.8 miles)
Time:	4hr
Altitude:	220m to 550m
Map:	IGN 1:25,000 2347OT (Quillan); Rennes-le-Château and Couiza are in map fold 5B

This walk begins at the Renaissance-style Château des Ducs de Joyeuse (now a classy hotel) (1), at the north end of Couiza, close to the junction between the Rivers Aude and Sals.

From the château, go to the right of the playing fields, turn left alongside the River Sals when you reach it and cross that river at some stepping-stones. ◀

If you prefer not to cross the river here there is a ford on the left a short distance further on, and just beyond that a bridge.

Turn left, go through the narrow streets of the town, pass to the right of a church, and emerge onto a small square. Turn right along the rue St Jean and reach the busy D118 main road through Couiza. Turn right here and walk along the footway on the opposite side of the road.

Just after passing a road bridge on the right, turn left (2) up a lane, signposted as a walking route up to Rennes-le-Château (2.5km). Keep to the main track as it winds up the hill, through woods and alongside open areas from where views back down to Couiza and the Aude valley occasionally appear.

After passing through a plantation of conifer trees, approach an open, fenced area with, perhaps, a lot of junk lying around. Turn right just before the entrance to that open area and climb alongside a fence to the edge of a cultivated field (may be ploughed in winter). From this point (3), turn right. Go right around the perimeter of the field, over to its opposite side. Follow the waymarked route where it turns half-right to leave the field and becomes a path through a conifer plantation. The path eventually meets a track where you turn right. Reach a T-junction of tracks (4) where you turn left.

Climb steadily on this track towards Rennes-le-Château, of which you soon have a splendid view. Even more striking, in clear weather, will be the view to the right across to the Pyrenees. The summits over 2000m stretch from plateau-like Madres due south (on the left) to the St-Barthélemy massif (on the right).

As the track levels out, look for a turning, sharp right, onto another waymarked path (5). Turn up that path; it will take you along the western edge of **Rennes-le-Château**. Pass under the Magdala tower and arrive in

The Tour Magdala in Rennes-le-Château, one of several elaborate constructions erected around 1900 by the parish priest, Saunière. His source of funds remains a mystery.

The fascinating church, presbytery and adjacent buildings of Rennes-le-Château, which are worth a visit, are at this end of the village.

a car park from where there is a magnificent view to the south. Here you will find a very helpful panel indicating the features you can see on a fine day, including (on the left) the Pech de Bugarach, the Matterhorn of Cathar castle country. ◀

Leave Rennes-le-Château by the minor access road at its eastern end. On leaving the village, this road swings sharply to the right (and you can cut off that loop by a short footpath). Then take a steep waymarked path which leaves the road and descends to the left, with dog kennels on the left. Near the bottom of that cobbled (and possibly slippery) path, fork left (leaving the yellow waymarks behind) and turn left onto the D52. Take care there on the blind corner. After going a little way along this road, take a steep cut-off path to the right, which brings you to the road intersection at point (6).

Go straight ahead, eastwards, along a small metalled road crossing an almost bare limestone plateau. From the crest of the ridge at the top of this road there is a view to the north down to **Coustaussa**, with its impressive remains of a Cathar castle. From here continue downhill along the metalled road for a short distance until you meet a farm track going sharp left (7).

Turn sharp left along the farm track. Go through a gate then turn right, following large, homemade, red-and-white signs (for Couiza & Coustaussa). These lead you all the way, northwards, down the hill along a winding, well-beaten – if occasionally slightly overgrown – path, into the Sals valley below. Be especially careful, shortly after beginning this descent, when you come to an open area. Your track meets another track coming from the left, then starts to bend to the right towards some beehives below. Shortly after that track junction you must turn off the track, left, onto a footpath.

Thereafter keep to the main path until, towards the bottom of the hill, you pass through a wooden gate (with a sign asking you to close it). Follow the jeep track ahead down to a vineyard near the bottom of the valley. There are magnificent views from this track across to Coustaussa, with its high but crumbling castle walls.

After passing to the right of the vineyard, turn right along a track which takes you to a ford, on the left, over the River Sals (8). Cross the ford and go up to the D613, a busy main road. It is safer from here (because you have a clearer view of oncoming traffic) to turn left, follow the roadside for 200m, then turn sharp right up a minor road signposted for Coustaussa.

Just before you reach a hairpin bend in this minor road, turn sharp left up a gravel track. This cuts off a section of the road. Then follow the road to the edge of the village. Fork left and follow the lane which skirts the village to the south. The remains of the castle (9) at the far, western end are in a state of disrepair, and notices there advise you not to get too close.

Go back through the village and, at its eastern end, turn left and follow a lane northwards to an intersection (10) with the scant remains of a small chapel on the right and a cemetery to the left.

From the intersection go straight ahead, uphill. A little later on, your route (yellow waymarks) forks left near the edge of scrubland. But first go a little further uphill to inspect a splendid, and perhaps exceptionally large, example of a **capitelle**, on the left (11). Go back down to the track fork and turn right there. You pass more *capitelles*, or the remains of them, on the way.

The waymarked route (a track here) forks left, then turns sharp left onto a path leading into scrub. The path bends to the right; not long after it turns to the left again, downhill. Where it forks lower down, go right. After a passage between low stone walls, the path becomes almost entirely overgrown. Scramble up a small embankment on the right onto the edge of a vineyard and continue to head in the same direction. Turn left at a track crossing in the vineyards, opposite a small stone cabin. You soon reach the road which you left at the cemetery, with a large building opposite (12). Turn right here.

Now follow the track you are on all the way downhill to Couiza. Rennes-le-Château can be clearly seen, high on the skyline to the left. You eventually reach the outskirts of Couiza. The road bends to the right, with open hillside directly ahead and with the Château des Ducs de Joyeuse coming into view below. Meet the main road through Couiza. Cross that, turn to the right and follow the tree-lined avenue back to the château (1).

POINTS OF INTEREST

Rennes-le-Château: The 'Bérenger Saunière Centre' is open to visitors throughout the year (except 1 January and 25 December). The centre includes the presbytery (now a museum), the Villa Béthania, the Magdala tower, adjacent gardens and the church. Exhibits relating to Saunière and the legend of the Cathar treasure are to be found in the museum. This building also contains some fascinating information and displays about the history of Rennes-le-Château and the surrounding area, from prehistoric times.

This site has for long been a magnet for tourists, but the number of visitors has shot up since the publication of the novel, *The Da Vinci Code* (which, like Rennes-les-Château, has among its focal points a character called Saunière and a mystery concerning the Holy Grail).

The *château* which gives Rennes-le-Château its name is on the site of the castle destroyed during the crusade against the Cathars. It was largely reconstructed in the 16th century, and is not open to the public.

Coustaussa castle: The walk passes close to the decaying but striking castle ruins at Coustaussa. The castle was constructed by the lords of Carcassonne in the 12th century. After Carcassonne fell to the crusaders' army in 1210, Coustaussa was abandoned and was taken by Simon de Montfort. Thereafter, according to Georges Serrus, the castle 'was inhabited until the early 19th century, when it was largely pulled down'.

Capitelles have been aptly described as looking like igloos built of stone. They are cleverly constructed drystone huts, used as shelters for shepherds or as storage places by people working in adjacent fields and vineyards. Some have evidently been recently restored.

Visiting time
For the church, museum, and surrounding grounds and buildings in Rennes-le-Château, allow at least 2hr. (Some people spend a lifetime there, looking for hidden treasure.)

One of the intriguing stone cabins –
capitelles – *near Coustaussa*

Further information

- Rennes-le-Château tourist office, 11190 Rennes-le-Château; tel: (00 33) (0)4 68 74 72 68; office.de.tourisme.rennes-le-chateau@wanadoo. fr; **www.rennes-le-chateau.fr**.
- Couiza tourist office, Route des Pyrénées, BP 5, 11190 Couiza; tel: (00 33) (0)4 68 74 02 51; pays.couiza@wanadoo.fr.
- Communauté de Communes du Pays de Couiza, point accueil tourisme: (0 33) (0)6 81 42 02 28; contact@pays-de-couiza.com; **www.pays-de-couiza.com**.
- The multimedia literature about Rennes-le-Château and its mysterious treasure is enormous. If you want to explore it (much in English), the bookshop in Rennes-le-Château is a good place to start: Atelier Empreinte, 11190 Rennes-le-Château; tel: (00 33) (0)4 68 74 26 71; librairie@atelier-empreinte.com; **www.atelier-empreinte.com**. See also: **www.rennes-le-chateau.com**, and **www.rennes-le-chateau.org**.

16 THE PECH DE BUGARACH: FINAL WALK, FINAL THOUGHTS

The Pech de Bugarach rises steeply to an altitude of over 1200m, the highest point in the Corbières hills. It is the focal point, the central watchtower, of Cathar castle country. The Pech de Bugarach is a hill which is trying hard to be a mountain – and with no little success.

The rugged, unmistakable profile of the Pech de Bugarach is visible from high ground in almost all parts of the region covered by this book. An ascent therefore makes for a splendid climax to a walking tour of Cathar castle country.

Two walks are described in this section. The first, the 'scrambler's circuit', is a very exciting circular walk linking the village of Bugarach (1) with the summit (8), and which takes the best part of a day to accomplish.

The Pech de Bugarach, as seen from the village of the same name, at the start of the scrambler's circuit

This walk curves around the base of the hill, then turns and heads for the summit up the very steep southern side of the Pech de Bugarach. That steep section – the *fenêtre* route, named after a distinctive 'window' in a rock face which you pass on the way up – is a magnificent scramble. In parts it is slightly exposed and not suitable for those who suffer from vertigo. In good weather there is no danger. It won't cause concern to anyone with experience of scrambling in the Lake District, Snowdonia or the Highlands of Scotland.

The second walk – the 'popular promenade' – is shorter and less demanding, but is still a very exhilarating route. It goes from the Col du Linas (10) to the summit and back, and avoids the steep, slightly exposed section on the scrambler's circuit.

PRACTICAL INFORMATION
Access to starting points
There is no direct route by road from Quillan to Bugarach, and all routes involve driving along winding and sometimes narrow country roads. Probably the best option is to go north from Quillan on the D118 main road to Couiza, then turn right onto the D613. Just past Coustaussa, turn right onto the D14 through Rennes-les-Bains and follow that all the way to Bugarach. The Col du Linas is a few kilometres east of Bugarach, on the D14.

Public transport in this area is scarce.

Navigation
The scrambler's circuit should be treated as a high mountain walk; it encouters scree, steep rocky slopes and boulder fields. Across such sections in particular the line of the path is not always clear and the waymarks may be tricky to spot in mist. Make sure that you can navigate with map and compass over such terrain before attempting this walk. Take great care not to knock stones and boulders onto the heads of those people following you; watch out for falling stones from above.

At the start the circuit follows the Sentier Cathare with blue and yellow waymarks. You leave that trail at point (6). From that point – and right over the summit and down to le Linas (11) – the route is indicated by yellow waymarks. You may also see some red and white waymarks on the scramble between points (6) and (8), but these are best ignored. From (11) back to Bugarach village, follow red and yellow waymarks.

The river crossing outside Bugarach village – at (2) – and the one just above the Cascades des Mathieux – between (3) and (5) – should normally present no

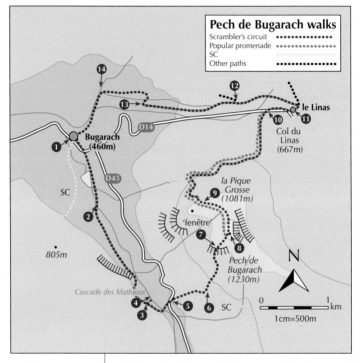

Pech de Bugarach walks

Scrambler's circuit	••••••••••••••
Popular promenade	••••••••••••••
SC	••••••••••••••
Other paths	••••••••••••••

If the rivers cannot be crossed, follow the D45 south of Bugarach. Re-join the scrambler's circuit at point (5).

problems, but they could be uncrossable during and shortly after heavy rainfall. ◀

Bear in mind that the summit is exposed, with long vertical drops on the east side in particular. Don't approach the highest point in strong winds.

Some sections on both routes can be muddy and slippery when wet, and are likely always to be so outside the summer period.

ROUTE DESCRIPTION – SCRAMBLER'S CIRCUIT

This walk starts in the centre of Bugarach, by the village church (1). Take the street leading out of the village to the southeast, heading for a valley just to the right of the Pech de Bugarach.

Distance:	13km (8.1 miles)
Time:	6hr
Altitude:	450m to 1230m
Map:	IGN 1:25,000 2347OT (Quillan); Bugarach village is in map fold 8C

As you leave the village, join the D14. Continue along that road in the same direction, but where it swings sharply to the left, go straight on, along an unsurfaced track signposted for the Cascades des Mathieux. You are now on the Sentier Cathare (blue and yellow waymarks).

The track passes to the left of a relatively new manmade lake. Where another path forks off to the left, carry straight on along your track, which also immediately goes uphill.

Beyond the head of the lake, the track descends. It crosses a river (2), which feeds the lake. Follow the track to the left after the river crossing, then fork right and start to climb again. Traverse the side of a hill through woodland, with the crags of the Pech de Bugarach looming high and fearsome on the left, above the other side of the valley. From here it is difficult to imagine how an ascent of the peak will be possible – but all will be revealed...

The track crosses some open ground, with a fine view straight down into the valley on the left. The river has undercut the slope on the other bank, and a great cross-section through the layered rocks above the river is visible.

The valley narrows and the track approaches cliffs on the right. It curls to the right, around a spur at the end of those cliffs. It then bends to the left. Shortly after that look out for a path which descends very steeply on the left (3) – see detour page 198. You are now above the Cascades des Mathieux.

Climb back up to the main track, and turn left along it. The track soon descends to the river higher up the valley, swinging to the left. Cross the river again, then

The path from (3) descends to one of the waterfalls. It is well worth making the detour – but take care on the slippery path. There are wooden handrails for most of the way. About two-thirds of the way down another path goes off to the right and descends to a delightful section of the river bed just above the waterfall. The main path continues to the bottom of the waterfall, at the back of a huge rock amphitheatre (4).

follow the path up the other side of the valley, through a gate which should be closed behind you. Follow the path as it winds uphill through woodland to eventually meet the D45 (5).

Cross the road and immediately climb up into box woodland on the other side. After a little way, the path crosses a track then almost immediately emerges into open country, with the south face of the mountain straight ahead.

The path climbs up the open ground, but instead of going straight up the slope goes slightly to the left. Look carefully for the waymarks in this section.

The huge buttress of la Pique Grosse is close by on your left. Do you recognise the profile of the ugly Duchess in *Alice in Wonderland*?

Looking through the fenêtre *high up on the rocky slopes of the Pech de Bugarach, Canigou mountain can just be seen, far to the south*

The path joins another one, and turns right along it for a short distance. Turn left off the Sentier Cathare to follow a path which is lavishly signposted for the summit (6). You may be able to see, high above towards the top of the mountain, a large hole in a cliff face: the *fenêtre* ('window'). In due course you will pass very close to that opening.

The path winds through the woodland above, with almost unremitting steepness. It eventually emerges into open country again, and ascends an extremely steep grass slope. You then reach the foot of a scree slope. The path – here with copious waymarks – zigzags up the scree.

Arriving at the foot of a cliff face, ascend a gully with rock steps, just to the left of that cliff. Boxwood bushes are on your left. You are now climbing among the crags and pinnacles which you could see shortly after leaving Bugarach. Further sections up rock staircases follow. Keep a close watch on waymarking at all times.

Approach the edge of the almost sheer east face of the mountain; you will glimpse, through a gap on the right, the valley far below. Traverse to the left, across a steep rock slope towards the *fenêtre*. This short section is slightly exposed, so take special care. As you approach the rib of rock jutting out below the *fenêtre*, it looks as if there is nothing but a great void just beyond it – but you cross that rib of rock onto a secure path which only becomes visible just before you set foot on it (7).

Immediately swing to the right and follow the path as it climbs the extremely steep, vegetation-covered slope which leads towards the summit. As you pass to the left of the *fenêtre* you may be able to look through it to the mountain of Canigou in the far distance.

It is a long haul from here to the summit of the Pech de Bugarach, but the path is clear and the trickiest sections of the climb are now behind you. The highest point is on an exposed mound, right on the edge of the hill's great east-facing cliff (8).

The magnificent view from the **summit** is more than ample reward for all the effort required to get here.

After leaving the highest point, return to and continue along the main summit ridge path as it now descends to the north. Bugarach village can be seen far below on the left, and the hamlet of le Linas – which you are heading for – is just over on the right.

The path swings round to the left to follow the line of a grassy shoulder. It then descends steeply into a woodland-covered section. Emerge into open ground again, and the path swings to the right. Here you reach the northern slope of the mountain.

At a path fork (9) go right (the path going straight ahead goes to the summit of la Pique Grosse). The route down to the Col du Linas, mostly in woodland, is now straightforward – well used, well waymarked and easy to follow. After a long, steep, winding descent, the path turns to the right and starts to rise again. But eventually it swings left to go down alongside an enclosed area of open land. It turns right, back into woodland, along the access track for that enclosure. ◀

At that right turn you may see a dilapidated example of something which is quite rare in this country: a sign, in French, stating 'No Entry. Beware of Bull'.

At a track fork just beyond the woodland, go down to the left. You soon reach the Col du Linas on the D14 (10). Turn right and follow that road for a short distance. Fork left off the D14 and go through the hamlet of le Linas (11). During the past couple of hours you will probably have seen various hand-painted signs advertising the refreshments available here.

When you reach the lane junction at the far end of the hamlet (just after passing, on your left, a building with the date 1681), turn left. Shortly after that you leave the hamlet behind and turn left again, onto an unsurfaced jeep track.

Continue westward along this track for a little way, with the Pech de Bugarach now on your left. Fork left down a grass track (12), signposted for Bugarach village. In the fields below, keep to the left. The path beyond has on both sides wire fencing which may be electrified. It goes along the spur of a hill. The path becomes more of a track and descends a little more steeply; then reaches a patch of semi-open ground, where it swings sharply to the right (13). It goes down into a wooded valley and swings sharp left, to cross a stream.

The sandy path now goes down the valley through enchanting woodland with moss-covered boulders and crags on either side. Where the stream on your left meets another coming down from the right, the path swings left (14). It soon emerges into open country. The stream on your right flows across a wide streambed of bare rock. Bugarach village is now ahead; cross a charming little stone bridge and enter the village.

When you reach a bar-restaurant on the right, turn left. The lane winds uphill, with the buttressed remains of a *château* on your right. Reach the village church and thus return to the start of the walk (1).

A welcome hostelry in Bugarach village, at the end of the scrambler's circuit

ROUTE DESCRIPTION – POPULAR PROMENADE

Distance:	6km (3.7 miles)
Time:	3.5hr
Altitude:	670m to 1230m
Map:	as for scrambler's circuit; the Col du Linas is in map fold 9C

From the Col du Linas (10) walk up the unsurfaced jeep track away from the road, as indicated by a sign for the summit at the start of the track.

Follow the track as it bends to the right, where another track comes in from the left. When you reach the bottom corner of fenced-off open ground, turn left up a path with the open ground on your right. A little further on follow the path where it turns right.

201

The path enters woodland and runs through it for some distance. For a while the path goes downhill, but it eventually bends to the left and start to climb seriously. For a long while the woodland obscures much of the view, but it affords some shade. You do not see the highest point of the Pech de Bugarach again (you could see it from the Col du Linas) until a later part of the walk, near the summit ridge.

Eventually you come close to the cliffs marking the upper part of the mountain – but there is still a lot of climbing ahead. Ignore a path going off right (to la Pique Grosse) and bear to the left (9). The highest part of the mountain then comes into view.

Climb steeply to the left, once more through woodland. You suddenly emerge onto a grassy shoulder, with the peak now clearly visible over on the right. Beyond the shoulder, follow the path round to the right, as it traverses a steep slope. You come closer and closer to the edge of the summit ridge on the left. A deep gully opens out to the left, and the exposed summit knoll, reached after a short scramble, is just to the right of that (8). The view from the **summit** is ultra-wonderful.

Return to the Col du Linas by the same route.

Further information
• Bugarach: la Mairie, 11190 Bugarach; tel: (00 33) (0)4 68 69 86 72; mairie@bugarach.fr; **www.bugarach.fr**.
• See also **www.pays-de-couiza.com** and **www.audetourisme.com/ pointBugarach**.

Some final reflections from
the summit of the Pech de Bugarach

This is the end of our tour of Cathar castle country. Much of the landscape we have traversed is now stretched out below the summit. For example, the rocky eminence on which Rennes-le-Château sits is clear to the northwest. On the northern horizon is the Montagne Noire, where Lastours is tucked away. The cliffs below Peyrepertuse castle are not far to the east. Only a few kilometres to the southwest lies the forest where Puilaurens castle is perched. Far to the west are the St-Barthélemy mountains above Montségur.

So this is a good spot from which to reflect on the story of the Cathars.

It is difficult not to shudder when recalling the immense cruelty and suffering imposed upon the Cathars , their followers and supporters. That cruelty is all the more repulsive because the Cathars demonstrated several aspects of the finer side of human nature – especially in their honesty, asceticism and solidarity in the face of brutal repression. It would be heartening to think that part of our generation's fascination with the Cathars is born of a respect for their good qualities and a desire to pay tribute to them.

But let us not over-romanticise them. Atrocities were committed by Cathar supporters too – and some of the Cathars' own doctrines and practices inflicted great cruelty on their followers, having more than a hint of the suicide pact about them. The Cathars were also convinced that they were right and that all other churches were wrong. In particular, they believed that the Catholic Church was the work of the devil. The Cathars were fundamentalists; no more so, perhaps, than the medieval Catholic Church, but one important question remains. Had the Cathars not been crushed, and had they become instead powerful and well resourced, would they have been as intolerant of any opponents as their oppressors? It's quite possible.

Nor should we delude ourselves that what happened to the Cathars is something restricted to the distant past. Dissent and peaceful challenges to the established order are still suppressed with great brutality in many parts of the world. Religious and other forms of fundamentalism still flourish, often bringing terror and destruction in their wake. Minority communities are still scapegoated and, in particular, anti-semitism is on the march again. Civil wars and crusades remain far from unknown.

But – at the very least – heretics are no longer being burned at the stake in Languedoc. After being a theatre of war and conflict for centuries – between Franks and Visigoths, Moors and Christians, Catholics and Cathars, French and Spanish, Nazi occupiers and Resistance heroes – the country at our feet is now

A corner of Lordat village

a place where peace has settled for good, or so it seems. The people who live there can devote themselves to much more agreeable activities – such as producing some of the world's most delicious wines, and weaving networks of waymarked trails that delight ramblers from many nations.

We can even hope that – since a permanent peace has now settled on this war-torn region, after two millennia of conflict – the same may be possible in those parts of the world where violent clashes still rage. In any event, for what we now perceive, here as elsewhere in Europe, let us be truly grateful – and let us not take this peaceable state of affairs for granted. We need to sustain it and to build upon it.

Meanwhile, shadows are lengthening on the Pech de Bugarach. We need to think about returning soon to lower ground. Before descending, we can gaze one last time on that wonderful horizon to the south. There, beyond the innumerable waves of the Fenouillèdes hills, stretches the long line of the high, serrated peaks of the eastern Pyrenees, from Canigou in the east to Roc Blanc, near Quérigut, further west. Those are the mountains of the Mediterranean sun, a land with its own history, its own legends and its own mysteries. The immense panorama has a cheerful message for us: there will always be more mountains to climb, and a new country to explore and to marvel at.

With that reassuring thought, we turn and descend – an optimistic spring in every stride.

APPENDIX 1

Useful addresses

French Travel Centre, 178 Piccadilly, London W1V OAL; tel: 09068 244123; info@mdlf.co.uk; **www.franceguide.com**.

Comité Départemental du Tourisme de l'Aude, Conseil Général, 11855 Carcassonne Cedex 9; tel: (00 33) (0)4 68 11 66 00; documentation@aude-tourisme.com; **www.audetourisme.com**.

Comité Départemental du Tourisme Ariège Pyrénées, 31 bis, avenue du Général du Gaulle BP143, 09004 Foix Cedex; tel: (00 33) (0)5 61 02 30 70; tourisme.ariege.pyrenees@wanadoo.fr; **www.ariegepyrenees.com**

The Aude and Ariège tourist departments can also supply (and list on their websites) the addresses and other details of all the local tourist information offices in their *départements* (the majority of local offices in Cathar castle country). Those are the best places for up-to-date information about accommodation, transport and taxi services, shops, market days, opening times of places of interest, special events, and so on.

In Paris
Fédération Française de la Randonnée Pédestre, 14 rue Riquet, 75019 Paris; tel: (00 33) (0)1 44 89 93 90; passion.rando@ffrandonnee.fr; **www.ffrandonnee.fr**.

In Carcassonne
Point Info-Rando FFRP Aude, Maison de Tourisme Vert, 78 ter, rue Barbacane, 11000 Carcassonne; tel: (00 33) (0)4 68 47 69 26; ffrp@carcazssonne.fr. This is a useful source of information about walks in Aude.

If you are surfing the Internet for information about Cathars and Cathar castles, try **www.cathars.org**. This website is entirely in French and at first sight looks a bit eccentric. Once you get into it you will find that it is a good source of, for example, castle opening times, prices of entry, relevant addresses, telephone numbers and websites. It also has several illustrations and plans of the castles.

APPENDIX 2

General publications

There is a huge amount of literature about the Cathars, in French, English and other languages. Many publications in French – walks guidebooks, general books, tourist guidebooks, special editions of glossy magazines, and so on – can often be bought in bookshops (*libraries*) and newsagents' (*Maisons de la Presse*) in and around Cathar castle country. More and more publications in English are being stocked in such outlets.

In Britain, several bookshops stock literature about Cathars and Cathar castles. On the Internet, **www.amazon.co.uk** is always worth searching. Even when books are currently out of print, you may be able to buy secondhand copies, usually at very reasonable prices, via Amazon.

In France, Fnac is a big bookshop chain. Their website, **www.fnac.com**, is also worth browsing, especially if you are looking for books in French that you cannot easily find outside France.

For literature about travel and walking in Cathar castle country, try the addresses and websites (IGN, Stanfords, and so on) referred to in the Introduction.

The publications mentioned below – many of which the author found useful in preparing this book – amount to only a tiny fraction of the relevant literature. They are all worth recommending, but it is not suggested that they are necessarily the best of what is available.

Several **guidebooks in French** describe walks in Cathar castle country. Where any of them are relevant to a particular walk, details are given in the corresponding section. Here it is worth noting in particular the *Topo-guides* published by the FFRP (see Appendix 1) and the *Sentiers d'Émilie* series. (The latter, published by Rando éditions, offers a selection of relatively short walks suitable for families with young children.) Those titles particularly relevant to Cathar castle country are:

- *L'Aude, Pays Cathare à pied* (FFRP *Topo-guide* PR, ref D011)
- *L'Ariège à pied* (FFRP *Topo-guide* PR, ref D009)
- *Le Pays de Foix à pied* (FFRP *Topo-guide* PR, ref P091)
- *Le Pays d'Axat à pied* (FFRP *Topo-guide* PR, ref P111)
- *Sur les traces des Cathares, le Chemin des Bonshommes* (FFRP *Topo-guide* GR107, ref 1097)

- *Les Sentiers d'Émilie en Pays Cathare*
- *Les Sentiers d'Émilie en Ariège*

The FFRP *Topo-guides* can be bought by credit card via, for example, the IGN and Stanfords websites, but not via the FFRP website.

Sections of the **Sentier Cathare** long-distance footpath are followed by some of the walks in this book. There is a guidebook in French to that trail, *le Sentier Cathare*, published by Rando éditions. Its price is about 15 Euros. It has excellent photographs and other illustrations of Cathar castles and the surrounding countryside, plus useful information about accommodation, the Cathars, the individual castles and so forth. The most recent edition was published in 2005. It is available in shops in France and via the Amazon and Fnac websites. A Cicerone guidebook in English to this trail is also currently in preparation.

A good **general tourist guide in English** to that part of France including Cathar castle country is *The Green Guide – Languedoc, Roussillon, Tarn gorges* (Michelin Travel Publications).

Very **readable books** in English **about the Cathars** include *The Perfect Heresy* by Stephen O'Shea (Profile Books) and *The Yellow Cross – the story of the last Cathars, 1290–1329* by René Weis (Penguin).

In French, the classic texts include *Histoire des Cathares* by Michel Roquebert (Perrin) and *Montaillou, village occitan* by Emmanuel Le Roy Ladurie (Gallimard). An English translation of the latter by Barbara Bray is entitled simply *Montaillou* (Penguin Books, 1978, reprinted 1990).

Anne Brenon is another leading authority on the Cathars. Her *Petit Précis de Catharisme* (Loubatières) is a gem: an erudite but clear and succinct portrayal of the Cathars' beliefs, history and social context.

Succinct, too, is *The land of the Cathars* by Georges Serrus (Loubatières). Translated into English from French, this is a richly illustrated, glossy publication which describes each of the Cathar castles. Just as well illustrated, but with a more detailed text about the castles (in French), is *Les plus belles balades en Pays Cathare* by Gilbert Roussel (Les Créations du Pélican).

Clear Waters Rising (a mountain walk across Europe) by Nicholas Crane (first published by Viking in 1996) is referred to more than once in this book. It didn't take him long to cross Cathar castle country en route for Turkey, but his account of that crossing is priceless.